FAT
BLOKE
SLIMS

FAT BLOKE SLIMS

HOW I LOST THREE STONE

BRUCE BYRON

MICHAEL JOSEPH
an imprint of
PENGUIN BOOKS

PENGUIN BOOKS

Published by the Penguin Group
Penguin Books Ltd, 80 Strand, London WC2R 0RL, England
Penguin Group (USA) Inc., 375 Hudson Street, New York, New York 10014, USA
Penguin Group (Canada), 90 Eglinton Avenue East, Suite 700, Toronto, Ontario,
Canada M4P 2Y3 (a division of Pearson Penguin Canada Inc.)
Penguin Ireland, 25 St Stephen's Green, Dublin 2, Ireland, (a division of Penguin Books Ltd)
Penguin Group (Australia), 250 Camberwell Road, Camberwell, Victoria 3124, Australia
(a division of Pearson Australia Group Pty Ltd)
Penguin Books India Pvt Ltd, 11 Community Centre, Panchsheel Park,
New Delhi – 110 017, India
Penguin Group (NZ), 67 Apollo Drive, Rosedale, North Shore 0632, New Zealand
(a division of Pearson New Zealand Ltd))
Penguin Books (South Africa) (Pty) Ltd, 24 Sturdee Avenue, Rosebank,
Johannesburg 2196, South Africa

Penguin Books Ltd, Registered Offices: 80 Strand, London WC2R 0RL, England

www.penguin.com

First published 2009
1

Copyright © Bruce Byron, 2009
All rights reserved

The moral right of the author has been asserted

Printed in England by Clays Ltd, St Ives plc

ISBN: 978–0–141–03850–6

The contents of this book have been carefully researched, but are not intended as a
substitute for taking proper medical advice. If you have any acute or chronic disease,
or are taking medication, you should always consult a qualified doctor or health practitioner.
The author and publisher accept no liability for damage of any nature resulting directly
or indirectly from the application or use of information in this book.

www.greenpenguin.co.uk

Penguin Books is committed to a sustainable future
for our business, our readers and our planet.
The book in your hands is made from paper
certified by the Forest Stewardship Council.

This book is dedicated to my beautiful Lily and Jack,
for supporting me the only way children know how –
with all their hearts; and to my lovely wife Tanya
without whom none of this would have happened.

CONTENTS

INTRODUCTION

I have to be honest. The idea for this book was my wife's. Tanya has been trying, unsuccessfully, for quite some time to bring my attention to my burgeoning weight. Her father died of a massive coronary and she didn't want to lose her husband the same way. That alone sounds like a very good reason to bring it up in conversation, but the subject of my weight has always been a touchy one and she knew that to approach it was tricky – I can be very defensive about the whole thing. But she took the bit between her teeth and said that I should try to lose weight and get fit not just for her and the kids, not just for myself, but also for all the other guys in my position. I should do it publicly in a news-paper column and book.

Why that didn't scare me straight back into my Fat Bloke shell, I don't know. Perhaps it was partly because I'm an actor and always seeking approval (being liked in print, yes please). But I think the real reason was that Tanya laid it out in a way that inspired me: it would be creative, it would be enlightening and informative. I could help myself and others at the same time. We had a laugh at the idea of checking out all the fad diets out there, faith healers, alternative weight-loss programmes, hypnosis, colonics and so on.

But there was no guarantee I would succeed. It could also be humiliating – what if Fat Bloke Slims became Fat Bloke Just Keeps Getting Fatter? On the other hand, maybe the fear of failing would keep me on the straight and narrow …

So, guess what? I took up the challenge. This is the documented journey of a soon-to-be-fifty-year-old, seriously overweight man who works long hours and wants to be around to see his children grow up, a man who wants to be able to play and do exciting strenuous activities with his family, and enjoy getting old with his beautiful wife. Basically, I want to be around long enough to enjoy the rewards of our very hard-earned life.

So where do you come in? Well, I hope that my journey is going to help others see what it takes to change for the better and for good. I'm going to talk about my life from being a fat child to skinny teenager to fat adult so you, and I, can see how learned behaviour is just that – *learned behaviour* that can be unlearned. None of us are big-boned or just built that way: the simple truth is that we eat and drink too much of the wrong things and don't do enough exercise. We don't know when to stop drinking wine or beer or eating everyone's leftover chips and we don't know how to listen to our bodies.

But why should you listen to me? After all, I'm no expert on weight loss or nutrition. I'm just an ordinary bloke who feels he's earned his dinner and a drink at the end of a hard day and who prefers not to go near a set of scales if he can possibly avoid it. But that, I think, is the key. If I can do it, anyone can, and the problems I run into will probably be the ones that *you* run into.

This isn't about me preaching a holier-than-thou, born-again, look-at-me-aren't-I-brilliant ethos. This is about me realizing that I'm overweight, that I don't want to be that way and deciding to do something about it. I want to be healthy, and I believe there are lots of blokes out there, just like me – fat, over forty and unfit – who are looking, with very little support from anyone, at trying to change their lifestyle. If that's you, and you can pick up this book and read it and get inspired, that's great. That's what I want.

But … a word of warning. If you're going to succeed, you have to be completely focused on what you want to do. You've got to make a decision that your life is going to change for good. Maybe this book will help you do that. But it's no quick-fix, miracle cure that will guarantee you lose weight. The durr factor is high in this – I'm not going to tell you anything you probably don't already know. I'm just going to set out clearly and easily why you should take that decision and stick to it. If you're like me, you're old enough to know that there are no magic diets. The secret is changing your attitude. That's not easy. As you get older, your metabolism gets slower and you're quick to gain weight and slow to lose it, so it's easy to become dispirited. But if you're not focused and prepared to stick with it, you'll never do it.

I believe I heard what Tanya was saying because I was ready to hear it, and this mindset will be key to my success. I believe that my father-in-law's death affected me more deeply than I realized and I woke up to just how much my children loved me and how much I wanted to be around to love them back. For the first time in my life I faced my mortality and it didn't just scare me, it motivated me. Without that motivation and a desire for change, I could not succeed, I'm sure of that.

I don't plan on being on a diet for the rest of my life. I don't plan on denying myself the pleasures in life. I plan on, for once, being honest with myself when I look in the mirror, and changing my life for the better, for ever.

Today's the day I stop making excuses.

I

HOW DID I GET HERE?

It is May 2007. I'm standing in front of the mirror, taking a good, hard look at myself. I've done this all my life, from the time I was just a kid. But this time it's different.

You see, I have a weight issue – the issue being that I have too much of it. My life has been a rollercoaster journey with my weight. I've been chubby and I've been thin as a pole in my time but, recently, over the past three years actually, there has been a rather obvious trend upwards.

Tanya, my wife, has been with me for a lot of this journey.

A number of things happened in the last few years which have, I think, contributed to my weight increase. In April 2005, our lives were shattered when my father-in-law died suddenly of a massive heart attack. That day, Tanya had been filming the television programme *The House of Tiny Tearaways*, and she received the news just as she was about to go into a consultation with a family.

I was on the other side of London filming an episode of *The Bill* when I got the call, and went straight home to be with our children, then aged seven and ten, while Tanya was driven immediately to Yorkshire to be with her mother. It was the day before Tanya's birthday and she was utterly devastated.

I had always been very close to Tanya's dad. In many ways he was closer to me than my own father, and his death hit me hard. The previous new year, Tanya and I had both given up smoking, and it was going well but, by the time the dust settled, when the funeral was over and we were trying to work out what to do with the estate and the mountains of paperwork, I was smoking at least a pack a day and drinking an uncomfortable quantity of wine just to get through the night.

I also became ill quite soon after these events and needed surgery and a long period of recuperation, during which I continued to smoke and drink. I went back to work too soon (good old Irish Catholic guilt) and became ill all over again. I was caught in a cycle of pain, ill health and stupidity, the likes of which I wouldn't wish on my worst enemy. My weight was creeping upwards and I felt dreadful. By the end of that awful year, it was time to make a fresh start. On New Year's Eve 2006, I decided enough was enough – I would quit smoking and get fit. I managed the smoking but, as far as getting fit was concerned, how could I? Like many men of my age, I regularly work over seventy hours a week. When am I supposed to exercise? When and how do I eat healthily? What can I do?

Well, back to May 2007, back to the mirror. I'm standing here because my wife has just told me it's time I did something about myself or she's going to lose her husband the same way she lost her father, and she doesn't want that, and neither do I. It's hard to hear it, but I know I've got to.

The bloke I'm staring at is about to turn forty-nine, he has a 40-inch waist and man boobs, and I can tell you that it's not a good look. I'm five foot seven and weigh 15 stone 12lb – that makes me morbidly obese. Those words are pretty depressing. Not only that, but most of the time I feel like crap. Perhaps it's because I do virtually no exercise and love to eat and drink, but I'm puffed out going up the stairs, I sweat during meals – the fat in my body acts as an insulator for hot food – and I'm constantly tired. How the hell did I get here?

Being fat has snuck up on me, in that insidious way it does, so now I am almost twice the man I was, and not in an heroic sort of way. Once, I could eat and drink hefty amounts and stay the same weight. Or I could hold off for a couple of days and fat would melt away. Not any more. Now, the weight gets on me and sits there stubbornly, refusing to move.

Like most blokes, I've made efforts to tackle it. I joined a gym. Actually, over the years I've spent so much on gym membership, I probably could have bought the gym by now. Every month I pay a subscription (£60) *just in case* I want to run on a machine (and I never seem to want to). In the process, I've made LA Fitness rich – over two years I've given them nearly £1,500, for nothing. That's what it would cost me to buy the iMac I covet but can't afford. It sounds nuts, doesn't it? I mean, would you really walk up to a stranger on the first of every month with £60 in your hand, and say, 'There you go, mate, have an iMac down payment on me'?

Of course you wouldn't – but that's what I'm doing and maybe that's what you're doing too. My gym money has left me nothing to show for it except for an extra roll around my middle.

Whenever I've felt fat and decided to lose weight, I've thrown money at the problem by spending a fortune on health equipment, get-fit kit, gizmos and gadgets from home treadmills to mountain bikes. I've carried on eating and drinking just the same but tried to build more exercise into my life. After a few enthusiastic weeks, I'd always tire of it and go back to my old ways.

Currently, in the UK, around six in ten men are medically defined as overweight. That's breathtaking, isn't it? Sixty per cent of us are overweight. What the hell's going on? And one in six of us is obese. Obesity in the UK has more than doubled in the past eighteen years and, among blokes, it's tripled. With this come increased risks to our health, including coronary heart disease – the UK's biggest killer. According to my friends at the British Heart Foundation, heart disease kills one in five males every year. It is responsible for 32 per cent of premature deaths in men. Someone dies of a heart attack every six minutes in the UK.

I'm staring at myself in the mirror and realizing the cold, hard truth: that could be me.

I don't want it to be me. There's too much good stuff going on to bow out now. I'm married to the love of my life, who's also three inches taller than me and gorgeous, I have two of the best kids I've ever met, a great home, brilliant friends and a dream career. The thing is, I want to be around long enough to enjoy what I've got, and the way I'm going, I won't be.

As I stand there, I realize that the game is finally up. It's time to change. I don't want be Brad Pitt, but I also don't want to be Johnny Vegas. And I need to be around to see my kids grow up. So it's time to do something about my weight and stop being fat. This time, I'm serious.

I start to draw up a plan.

❑ I want to lose three stone to take me down to my ideal weight, 12 stone 12lb. (The last time I was that weight was in the late eighties, so it will be no mean feat.)

❑ I want to do it in a healthy and sustainable way. There's no point in crash-dieting and then putting it all back on again. I want a new way of eating and drinking that I can live with for good, so it can't be too rigid or self-denying – or else I'll just give in, I know I will.

❑ I want to get fitter, so I'm going to make time to go to the gym, ideally twice a week. And I'm going to work out ways to get more enjoyable exercise into my daily life, so it doesn't feel like a chore.

❑ I'm going to have a thorough health overhaul, so I understand exactly what's wrong with me and how I can fix it.

So far, so easy. But actually doing it will be the hard part.

I'm serious about losing weight, but that doesn't mean I've gone all holy and virtuous. I'm not going to sit in a group and cry about my fat inner child. I just want to sort out my fat outer bloke. And I want to enjoy it and have a laugh. The last thing I want to do is sob into my low-fat cheese and tomato sandwiches and hate every minute of the whole thing. Life is too short. There are too many good things out there to enjoy.

You know what? I reckon I can bust my guts. I'm going to do my best anyway. Let's see what happens.

2

GETTING STARTED

Tanya is delighted that I'm going to sort myself out, and she says she'll support me every step of the way. This is good news, because when you're part of a family it's not that easy suddenly to start living and eating differently to everybody else. Unlike many blokes, I'm involved in our food shopping and also turn my hand to a lot of the cooking (I know, a man of many talents ... Jamie Oliver, watch out), so it's going to be relatively easy for me to make sure that we buy and cook the kind of food that will help me lose weight.

If you'd like some information about some good things to stick in your weekly shopping basket, turn to p. 179, where I've written some ideas. You can either go shopping yourself or pass it on to whoever does the shopping in your house. Hopefully, like me, you'll have someone on hand who wants you to lose weight and get fit. Back-up will be vital!

Tanya and I sit down and take a good look at my diet. This is a typical food intake for me on a work day:

Fat Bloke's Pre-Life-Change Menu

❏ **5.30 a.m.** Have a cup of tea.

❏ **7.30 a.m.** Breakfast – in the work canteen. I'll have a cup of tea, two slices of toast (white or brown), margarine and, sometimes, tinned tomatoes on it; or I'll make a bacon and marmalade sandwich (try it, it's great), or have poached eggs on toast with tinned tomatoes. Besides cooked breakfast, there are also cereals, yoghurts and porridge on offer, but no fresh fruit.

❏ **10.30 a.m.** Tea and biscuits – there is nothing else on offer, so I usually end up scoffing some biscuits.

❏ **1 p.m.** Lunch – this will also be in the work canteen, or else in a catering facility on location. I'll eat meat – lamb, steak, ham or chicken – or fish, and vegetables or salad. In the winter, I might have a stew or a meat pie. For pudding, I'll have a fruit salad; and I'll drink a glass of water.

❏ **4 p.m.** Cup of tea. Sandwiches are offered, too, and I'll eat those if I'm hungry.

❏ **8–9 p.m.** Home at last. A couple of big glasses of wine, and then I'll eat supper: meat or fish with potatoes or pasta or rice, vegetables and salad. While I'm eating, I'll finish off the bottle of wine and occasionally open another with the wife, or even on my own if she doesn't feel like it. I don't usually eat pudding, but I might have some fruit. Once a week, we'll have an Indian takeaway: kormas, rice, naans, poppadoms – the works – and lashings of beer (not the ginger kind).

❑ Late-night post-wine sugar cravings sometimes catch up with me, and I'll open some ice cream or something and have a quick graze while I watch the telly.

Well, we look at my typical food day and think that, overall, it doesn't look too bad. I'm not scarfing vast amounts of fried food, cakes and chocolate, so that's a bonus. My diet is strong on protein, fruit and veg, but some obvious problems leap right out at me …

❑ I'm eating two large cooked meals a day. I only need one main meal, either in the middle of the day or in the evening, not two.

❑ I'm probably eating too many snacks without realizing it, because they're there or because I get the urge and don't say no to myself.

❑ I am definitely drinking a bit too much. You probably noticed that yourself.

❑ I'm not doing any exercise to balance the comfortable amount of food I'm packing away.

Result? I'm fat, and getting fatter.

How Does Fat Bloke Plan a Diet?

I am a man, there's no getting round that, and there are certain things I'm not going to do. I'm not going to be counting calories, weighing out miniature slices of cheese or noting down every little thing that passes my lips. It just ain't going to happen. The key to this whole thing, I think, is understanding yourself and not setting yourself unrealistic tasks that you're just going to fail at. If I have to keep a food diary or count up how much I'm eating every day, I just won't do it. I might for a day or two, or even a week or two. Then I'll stop and feel I've failed. That's my opinion at the moment, anyway.

The only way to diet is to start as I mean to go on.

So that means a sensible eating plan that's going to help me lose weight over the long term, rather than the short term.

I decide that my diet plan is not going to be crazy. It's not going to cut out one whole food group, or make me live on air and hot water, or allow me only starvation rations. Using the diet and nutrition information I've gleaned over the years from books, papers and magazines, I reckon I know enough about what a sensible diet is to draw one up for myself. So here goes ...

Fat Bloke's Forbidden Foods
(for now at least)

❑ **Refined sugars.** This is CRUCIAL. Refined sugars are the work of the devil and probably responsible for the obesity of the western world. Modern diets are saturated with them, and not just in the form of cakes and biscuits and sweets (though we're bombarded with plenty of those as well). Refined sugars have crept into all processed foods. Not only are they highly calorific but they have zero benefit nutritionally. It may sound blindingly obvious, but chocolates, ice creams, sweets, cakes and all that stuff have to go, preferably for good.

That would have been harder a while ago, when I had a really sweet tooth, but I'm not so keen on all that stuff now. I find it's easier to turn down sugar-heavy puddings, and I can indulge my desire for sweetness through fruit.

❑ **Bad carbs:** bread, potatoes, white rice and pasta. For years, dieters were urged to eat masses of carbohydrates and go easy on protein and fats. But despite all that low-fat, high-carb eating, the western world has gone on getting fatter. Now, we see the difference between good carbs – unrefined grains, whole cereals and other slow-release energy foods – and bad carbs that are high in sugar and give us short, unsustainable boosts of energy and then a corresponding dip downwards. Unfortunately, I consider bread, potatoes and pasta guilty parties and, while I'm trying to lose weight, I'm going to cut them out completely. Later, I'll eat them but in moderation. I mean, I'm never going to eat wholewheat pasta – I do not like that stuff at all, healthy or not, to the point where I'd rather not eat pasta at all. So, if I do eat pasta, I'll eat the good sort, but only occasionally. I avoid white rice where I can and have Camargue rice from France, wild rice, couscous, or cracked wheat instead. These are all slow-release good carbs that deliver great taste and fill you up.

❑ **Dairy.** We now understand a lot more about good fats and bad fats and, sadly, dairy contains a lot of the bad stuff – i.e. saturated fats – so we have to be careful about how much of it we take in. While I'm losing weight, I'm going to avoid it, apart from semi-skimmed milk, low-fat yoghurts and the occasional piece of cheese. After all, we do need fats and the calcium in dairy products, so it would be foolish to cut them out altogether.

❑ **Processed food.** High in salt, fat and sugar, these foods are no nos. Luckily for me, I don't eat much processed food or many ready-meals, but I know a lot of people do. They're addictive because they are highly flavoured, and home-cooked food (not stuffed with salt and sugar to make it taste of something) can sometimes seem bland afterwards. You've got to retrain your tastebuds. They've been bludgeoned half to death with processed foods, and will take a few weeks to rediscover real, natural tastes. Don't lose heart – your whole body will thank you for cutting out that overdose of salt and avoiding the hidden horrors of fat and sugar.

Fat Bloke's New Resolutions

❑ I'm going to start the day with a hearty breakfast of good carbs and fruit.
❑ I'm going to drink lots of water.
❑ I'm going to eat one main meal a day.
❑ I'm going to take my own lunch and healthy snacks into work whenever possible.
❑ I'm going to keep an eye on my portions.
❑ I'm going to drink less in the evening.
❑ I'm going to start exercising.

Like I said, it's not rocket science.

I'm convinced that I don't need to follow some kind of 'diet', join a dieting self-help group, or turn to acupuncture or listen to special DVDs to make me lose weight. I don't buy all that stuff. All I want to do is take control of my own eating my own way. Like lots of blokes, I want to know what the problem is and then solve it in the most logical way I can. So using a bit of common sense must be the right way.

And, anyway, what I haven't mentioned is that I've been this way before, a long time ago. And, right now, memories of what happened when I was a kid are flooding back ...

3

GROWING UP

This isn't the first time I've been fat. When I was nine years old, I weighed 12 stone – not far off the ideal weight for a grown man of five foot seven. I hadn't always been fat – quite the opposite. Until the age of seven, I was so skinny my mother was worried about my eating habits. Then, suddenly, I ballooned.

So my mother, as advised by the family doctor, took me to Weight Watchers.

I cannot now, as a parent, envisage being in a position where I would have to go down that route with my children. You could argue that it was the sixties and people were somewhat ignorant about the effects of being overweight, as they were of the effects of smoking, but whatever the thoughts surrounding obesity in adults, surely no one could have possibly imagined that it was okay to let kids get fat. I can tell you now, if you haven't been there, that being the fat kid is a bloody miserable experience. Apart from the constant teasing, your schoolmates laughing at you and girls not liking you, you couldn't run in football (I was regularly in defence, as though that's a place to hide and not be fit – hmm, I think the great John Terry would have a few words to say about that). I suffered from fallen arches, chafed thighs in winter and excruciating sweat rash in summer. I perspired when I ate and still do to this day. Why the fuck would anyone think it's okay to let a child go through that?

I know why it happened. My mother came from a family with eighteen children and in 1920s rural Ireland, food was at a premium. Her family grew what they ate, and there wasn't much of it – with seventeen other kids round the table, you've got to get in quick. As a result, in 1960s Fulham, my mum stuffed me with food to show me she loved me. At first, I was a fussy eater and often refused food, so she'd cook three or four meals to tempt my appetite and, eventually, my appetite responded in spades. On top of that, I had daily treats and sweets. My mother worked for John Mars in Slough at the time and every week all the employees would be given their ration of sweets. Sometimes my mother brought home so much that the top shelf of our pantry would be filled with these rolled-top white-paper bags. She would give large quantities to the local foster home every week, but I can assure you there was still lots left to get stuck into and, as an only child, I had no one else to share it with.

So I began to get fat (surprise, surprise).

My mum, a great mum then and still now, was hugely protective and told me I had big bones. So I grew up hating not just my bones but my entire body. I also hated being picked on.

Then it was off to Weight Watchers. My mother and I went to a large room every Thursday night (I can't honestly remember which night it was, I've wiped it from my memory, but Thursday rings a bell), where I was surrounded by fat, middle-aged housewives. I was not just the only child, I was also the only male. I sat there, waiting to be weighed in like a professional boxer in front of the assembled heavyweights. One after the other, everybody climbed on the scales in front of the entire room to have their weight announced. Those who had lost their quota or more were lavishly praised, while those who hadn't lost, or had even gained, climbed off the scales to a deafening silence.

I had to remove my shoes and track pants to get on the scales, and then it was the moment of truth. I was only a kid, and the weight came off me fairly quickly, so when my weight was called out, I would get congratulated for being the biggest loser. The irony was apparent to me even aged nine because, at school, I was definitely the biggest loser: the fat kid, rubbish at sport, the one no one wanted on their team. And now that I was on a special diet, I had to go into a classroom at lunchtime and eat on my own while everyone else was in the dining room. Afterwards, I would join the others in the playground, pretending that nothing was out of the ordinary. But of course it was. I was different, because I was fat.

Even at home, I was different. I ate special meals while my parents still tucked into the same food as usual. I mean, why wouldn't they? After all, they weren't fat. In fact, my mother was grossly *under*weight and my father, having been in the army for a number of years, was very fit and muscular. So I alone ate according to the rigid regime dictated by the diet sheet. Everything was weighed and measured exactly, therefore, if I stuck to it, I couldn't not lose weight. But, Christ, was it boring! And there was the stigma. I couldn't eat anything that wasn't prepared at home or by someone else on the same diet – pretty limiting, wouldn't you say? – and everyone knew it. At home, at school, I was the kid locked into his lonely fat life.

All of this did nothing to change my love of food and, back then, I felt constantly hungry and deprived. I remember volunteering to clear my parents' plates and, in the secrecy of the kitchen, wolfing down whatever leftovers there were, stuffing it in so fast in case they caught me doing it that I nearly choked. It feels as if I have been eating like that ever since. Up until recently, if I was still feeling peckish after a meal, I would go out to the kitchen to make a drink of some sort and quickly snuffle down a few whatevers, hiding the fact that I was eating, ashamed of it. The Jesuits used to say, 'Give me a boy till he's seven, and he's mine for life.' Perhaps there's some truth in it. When I was seven, I blueprinted my eating for the rest of my life.

My diet foods from that time remain two of my greatest hates: cheese and tomato sandwiches, and Tab Cola, a sugar-free soft drink. I recently looked up Tab online and discovered that it was sweetened with cyclamate but, after cyclamate was banned by the US Food and Drugs Administration in 1969, saccharine was used instead. Then, in 1977, saccharine was cited as a possible cause of cervical cancer, so Tab had to carry a health warning. How sweet. Nowadays, it's sweetened with saccharine and aspartame (another delightful chemical). No wonder I hate the stuff.

So there I am, drinking Tab, eating weighed and measured meals, sneaking leftovers off my parents' dinner plates and going to meetings of the local Weight Watchers. Eventually, I reached my target weight and stopped going, but my reward was to be photographed and interviewed by the local paper (I am recorded as saying I was bullied at school because I was fat), and that went on the front page of the paper.

If I thought I was bullied before the article, it was nothing to what happened afterwards. I mean, who quotes a nine-year-old verbatim like that?

My early experience of being fat gave me a self-hatred I've wrestled with ever since. I know – a strange admission for someone who became an actor and has made his living appearing on television. My whole job is about being looked at, even though I can't bear to look at myself. There's probably something deeply Freudian going on there.

As I grew up, I got thinner, and then fatter again, as my weight see-sawed up and down over the years. In my early twenties, I played music professionally and I wasn't much interested in eating – or sleeping, come to that. I was stick-thin for a while, and then I put on some weight. I remember thinking I was fat then, although photos from that period show that, in fact, I'm a normal size. Call it distorted body image, if you will. Having been a fat child, I was destined always to be miserable and dissatisfied with my body.

Then, in my mid-twenties, reality caught up with psychology when I really did hit the big time. Possibly – okay, probably – it was the alcohol. I became disillusioned with the music world and left it behind for a completely different life – the oil and gas industry. I left Britain and took a job working in a gas field in the South Australian desert. The contrast was just extraordinary: from noisy, crowded London to vast stretches of empty, dry land and solitary, physically demanding work. A bit of a shock for a boy from Fulham.

I discovered hard work and the amazing camaraderie between men working together. Lots of them were very tough guys, most enormous and tattooed, some ex-jail-birds. Yes, it was a colourful time in my life. The hard work meant that I began to bulk out with muscle and I became extremely fit. I'd grown a bit podgy and soft living in the city and drinking lots of beer. On the rigs, I became strong and well-built – at one point I had an eighteen-inch neck, and that was all muscle. It was great, but the downside is that all of that is waiting to turn to fat if you don't maintain it and, once you're off the rigs, it's not easy to stay that fit. What's more, drinking every night is a national pastime in Australia, and I took to it like a duck to water. It didn't show much at first – I was young, fit and working hard, and I was bulking out anyway. Later, I learned that the habit of drinking a lot and often will result in the accumulation of lard.

In my late twenties, the oil industry offered me huge opportunities, but I made the decision to get out. I'd had enough, and I knew I didn't want to spend the rest of my life working in dangerous, strenuous situations. It was time to listen to a little voice inside me that was telling me that, actually, all I'd ever wanted to do in life was act.

I can remember exactly when I was bitten by the acting bug. I was about nineteen years old and it was Christmas Day. We were all in the living room in the post-meal slump, half of us asleep, and I was trawling through the channels (not many of them in those days) looking for something interesting on the telly. I came across, of all things, Laurence Olivier in Shakespeare's *Richard III*. Quite simply, I was mesmerized. It was the best example of a gangster movie I'd ever seen, and Olivier was amazing. I thought, *I want to do that*.

Later, in my early twenties, I shared a house with some actors and watched enviously as they went off to drama school but, for some reason, I did nothing about it. Then, at the age of twenty-eight, I thought, *If I don't do this now, I never will*.

I turned my back on the lucrative world of oil for a life of penury and went to university in Australia. I slimmed down again, this time because I was so poor I couldn't afford to eat or drink much, and I had a part-time job in, of all things, a wine shop, where I worked hard lugging crates and bottles.

Then, fate took a hand, and one of those life-changing moments happened. I was putting in an English assignment when I came across a brochure that the tutor in charge had ordered for her daughter. It was for a drama school in Britain which had just opened and was looking for students. Just the thing for me, I thought, and I applied and was accepted. In December 1989, I came back to Britain to start a year-long drama course which I hoped would equip me for life as a professional actor.

To say I was cold in Britain was an understatement. I'd spent a number of years in the desert, and my thermostat was well adjusted to Australian heat. I headed to Scotland before my course started (the coldest place in the world, or so it seemed to me), where I shivered miserably, hugging radiators and wearing women's tights under my jeans in an effort to keep warm. Then I went to Yorkshire (the second-coldest place in the world) to start my drama course. I was shrivelled up by the climate and wondering what the hell I'd done.

In fact, I'd done the very best thing I possibly could have. The school was an amazing place, and the course was tough, packing three or four years' work into just one. I lost more weight, burning it off keeping warm and working hard. We did theatre productions, music, film, dance, movement, learning camera technique and sound processes and everything we could possibly need in our future acting careers. The aim of the school was to get its actors working, and it was extremely successful: 94 per cent of graduates found work, a stunning result by any standards. So, after my hard-working year, I graduated and moved to London. By then, Tanya and I were together, and I began trying to kickstart my career. It wasn't easy at first, and my weight began to climb because, if I wasn't working, I was bored and depressed: in my book, two of the surest ways to get fat.

Then I started working, and I loved it. Acting was exactly what I wanted to do and, gradually, I got bigger and better roles on TV and in film and theatre. Tanya and I got married, settled down, had kids. I was content, and now there was lots to celebrate and enjoy in life: a lovely wife, beautiful children, good friends and, of course, food and drink. Slowly, slowly, my weight climbed further and further upwards. I could often arrest it or take some off with a quick burst of activity and cutting back a bit on this and that but, as I got older and my metabolism slowed down, I couldn't lose weight quite as fast, or as easily. The lard was creeping inexorably on.

Five years ago, I got the role of DC Terry Perkins on *The Bill*, and it's been a fabulous experience. But the hours are long and intense and, when I'm not working, I feel the need to switch off and relax. I fell into the habit of opening a bottle of wine nearly every night. With Tanya's career taking off, she had stints away from home, and I'd often come in late to a quiet house with the kids and the au pair asleep, slump down in front of the telly with a bottle and some dinner and watch crap just to relax. Sometimes, I'd find myself crawling into bed at one in the morning, knowing I had to be up in four hours and wondering why the hell I did it to myself. And then, one day, I realized I was over fifteen and a half stone and creeping up to sixteen, and I knew it all had to change.

So, my relationship with my body and my weight is complicated. But I'm not alone, I know that. Most people are dissatisfied with one aspect or other of themselves.

The great thing about weight is that you can do something about it – you *can* change. I'm more determined than ever that I'm not going back to be that fat kid.

4

THE FIRST STEPS

Okay, time to assess the damage. If you're thinking of losing weight, and you know you're not in prime condition, the best thing to do first off is visit your GP for a physical MOT. Your doctor will be able to make sure you're fit to start a diet and fitness regime (though, to be honest, he or she will probably start cheering and clapping and telling you not to waste a moment getting on with it).

I'm ready to face the truth, so off I head to a British Heart Foundation (BHF) risk assessment centre.

These guys are great. Their simple aim is to prevent as much heart disease as possible, especially premature deaths, through pioneering research and vital prevention activity. They also help and support those who are already suffering the effects of heart disease. You can rock up to their centres (there are a handful of these on the move around the country – see their website at www.bhf.org.uk) and, free of charge have an assessment to estimate your risk of developing coronary heart disease, get your blood pressure, cholesterol and glucose levels tested. (You can, of course, also ask your GP for these tests.)

This is a great, if scary, way to start your push for a healthier you.

After the tests are complete, the BHF nurse will give you a breakdown of what needs your immediate attention and how to go about it.

I sit through the gamut of tests, slightly nervous about what the results are going to be. I feel like a teenager waiting for exam results, aware that I've not been as good as I could have been. I mean, I'm three stone overweight – they're hardly going to pat me on the back, tell me I'm doing fantastically and just to keep on the way I'm going.

The good news comes first, with my cholesterol results. Cholesterol is a type of fat found in the body. It's essential for good health, but too much of it in the blood is a bad thing, as it can clog up the arteries and hinder blood flow, resulting in heart attacks, strokes and blood-vessel problems. Seven out of ten people over forty-five have high cholesterol, and experts believe it's caused by the usual suspects: a bad diet high in saturated fats, lack of exercise and too much drinking, as well as family history and just being overweight in the first place. Cholesterol in the blood is measured in units called millimoles per litre of blood, and current UK guidelines recommend a total cholesterol level under 5mmol/l. Mine comes in at 3.5mmol/l, so I'm doing well.

But then the bad news … Body Mass Index results first, and they're not pretty. BMI is a simple calculation, based on your weight and height, to determine if your weight is within the healthy range. If you want to find out your BMI, you can either work it out yourself by dividing your weight in kilograms by your height in metres squared, ask your doctor to work it out for you, or go to a BMI calculator on the internet. You'll find one on the NHSDirect website at www.nhsdirect.nhs.uk (put 'BMI calculator' into the search box and it will come up).

On the Body Mass Index, you ideally want to score between 20 and 25, which shows you're a normal, healthy weight. Over 25 is 'overweight', and over 30 'obese'. I come in at 34. Oops. My waist is 40 inches, 3 inches more than the official maximum for me.

And I have high blood pressure.

These stats are bad news. The very kind nurse tells me that, if I don't improve them, I have a 21 per cent chance of a heart attack or stroke in the next ten years.

I leave the BHF centre, shaken and distinctly frightened. Those numbers have hit home. The nurse has spelled out what I knew anyway, but it's good to hear it from an impartial professional: I need to lose weight, improve my diet and exercise if I want to reduce my chances of dying of heart disease.

It helps me make the mental shift I need to make, without which I'm doomed to fail.

I'm completely determined – from here on in, it's a healthy diet and lots of exercise all the way. Fat Bloke is going to slim.

Time to Start Moving ...

It's the first week of my new regime, and I hit the ground running – literally. I decide I'm going to get fit as quickly as I can and, as usual, I'm full of enthusiasm. I'm going to start going to the gym not once, not twice, but three times a week.

The gym is a two-minute bike ride from the house, and I've been a member of it for years but, as I said, I've been feeding my iMac fund into it with very little return. All that's going to change now. The question is, what am I going to do when I get there? I've got a hazy idea of what I need to do, but how effective is that going to be? I want to use the time I've got to the best advantage.

Tanya has been using a personal trainer at the gym, and she tells me that he is a great motivator and really helps to keep her fit. She recommends I use him, for a while at least.

I know, I know ... personal trainers. It sounds a bit lala-land. What self-respecting celeb doesn't have their personal trainer? Madonna, Gwyneth ... and now me? I wasn't sure it was quite my scene, but Tanya said, 'Look, it's about beginning strongly and going on in the way that's going to be most beneficial to you. I know you, and you'll start off keen, but you'll just quit. If you're with a trainer, you'll do more than you would on your own – he'll push you on and encourage you to work at it. You've got hardly any spare time, so you've got to use the time you've got to the best advantage.'

I knew she was right, so I decided to go for it.

Okay, at this point, I can hear a collective laugh. *'That's all right for you, Fat Bloke. You can afford a personal trainer. What about the rest of us?'*

Yeah, I've thought about that. I'm in a very lucky position. I can afford to pay a trainer thirty or forty quid a session, but I'm well aware that lots of people can't. I don't want to sound as if I'm lecturing, but I have looked into alternatives for those who can't shell out for a trainer all to themselves, and you'd be surprised how many opportunities there are if you look into it. See the list below for some ideas about what you can do to get cut-price professional advice, and free fitness training ...

❑ Go to your local council-supported gym or leisure centre. They will have off-peak deals and discounts for low-income membership. They'll also have trainers there who can take you through the equipment, show you some exercises, draw up a plan for you and help monitor your progress.

❏ See if you can find two or three friends to share the cost of a trainer. Forty quid for one person is a lot, but ten or fifteen is a lot more reasonable and you'll get just as much out of it. Also, training with friends is a great motivator not to drop out or miss sessions.

❏ Go to some classes at the gym. There are plenty on offer, from high-impact aerobics and body shaping to gentler varieties of flexibility and strength work.

❏ Take up running in your local park: it's free, and good for you. Start off small – a five-minute run one day, a seven-minute run the next. Take it at your own pace until you can manage thirty to forty minutes, with ten- to twenty-second sprints every ten minutes. Finish with some stretches and even some push-ups or squats if you're feeling bold enough.

❏ Look for the circuit equipment in your local park: it will look like weathered wooden structures or planks on the ground. It's actually a useful and totally free exercise aid.

❏ Get a pedometer (they're cheap and available in sports shops) and try and make sure you're walking a minimum of 10,000 steps a day. Aim for 12,000, and then build up to 16,000 if you can.

❏ See if there is a Green Gym in operation near you.

This is a way to get some great outdoor exercise while helping the environment. The organizers will set you to work maintaining a public outdoor space such as a nature reserve: good honest hard work with a great result. Fun, too. Go to www2.btcv.org.uk/display/greengym for more information.

❑ British Military Fitness. If you can't afford a trainer but know you need discipline to start and carry on, try this. The army runs fitness classes in local parks all over Britain. They do cost, but they're relatively cheap ... certainly more affordable than a trainer and some gym memberships. You can find them on the internet at www.britmilfit.com or call 0870 241 2517. And you get a free trial class to see if it's for you.

❑ Don't forget low-impact, enjoyable exercise that you can build into your life – a swimming session, a brisk walk in the park, a bit of cycling. You'll feel so much better afterwards, I promise you. Exercise is nature's cure for lethargy, tiredness, depression, stress ...

❑ Remember that this is your health and it's worth investing in it if you possibly can. Did you see that bloke recently who won the lottery but who's suffering from advanced heart disease? He said he'd swap all the money in an instant if he could have his health back. Makes you think ...

I'm not exactly a gym virgin when I arrive there for my first session with Imran, soon to be known to me by the snappier name of 'The Bastard'. I used to do a lot of exercise in the past. Besides my strenuous work on the oil rigs, I used to box and run – I did a ten-kilometre run for Centrepoint a few years back – and I love mountain biking. I've also turned up for the occasional sweaty workout whenever I've been feeling guilty about overindulging, and know my way round the kit there. If you don't, please don't let that stop you. None of it is exactly astrophysics, and instructors are there precisely to make sure you can use the equipment safely.

In the changing room, I have a good look at myself in the mirror, reminding myself of exactly why I'm about to put myself through this. I'm not looking forward to it – in fact, I'm dreading it. But the sorry state of my reflection helps to focus the mind. 'You are so overweight, look at you,' I tell myself strictly. 'Force yourself to do this. If you don't, you will fail. It's a simple equation. Imagine what you want to look like. This is the way to get there.'

With those stern words ringing in my ears, I know what I have to do.

Imran isn't there to swap pleasantries with me, and we quickly get down to business. He assesses my fitness first, putting me through some stretches and then on to the running machine, where I start pounding away.

Then he starts talking to me, the idea being that if you can maintain a reasonable conversation over fifteen minutes while jogging, you're doing quite well.

I might be a bit rusty, but my body seems to have a fairly good memory, and I manage to get to the end of my run, although I am somewhat out of breath and sweaty.

'Mmm,' says Imran critically. 'You're quite fit but you're overweight, so we're going to concentrate on cardio and boxing, to burn fat.'

He immediately starts me boxing. After he's got me into the gloves, he shows me the uppercut, the jab and the cross. Then he puts some large pads on to his hands and makes me start throwing body shots into the pads, so that I'm jabbing and punching as hard as I can while the pads take the impact. Then he puts some combinations together – hook, hook, jab; cross, duck, cross – and we carry on until I'm breathless. There's a tiny pause for me to regain my breath and then I'm off again, this time running round the room as fast as I can. Then he starts throwing balls for me to run and get and bring back to him. I'm constantly changing directions, constantly moving. This is cardio. The whole idea is for me to get out of breath and for my heart rate to rise to a point where I start to burn fat for energy.

He keeps me moving for an hour and, by the time we've cooled down with stretches, I'm soaked to the skin, bright red in the face and utterly puffed out. To be frank, I feel awful.

But mentally I feel great. I feel triumphant. I've just done an hour of solid hard work, the first steps in my serious attempt to lose weight. I'm determined to carry on. I'm going to do this for a minimum of two sessions a week and, when I'm not doing that, I'm going to go to the gym for a run on the treadmill. It won't be easy, and I know that plenty of times I'm not going to want to – but I keep using that strict voice on myself – YOU'VE GOT TO DO IT.

If you want to do it too – and there about a million reasons why you should, besides losing weight – see my guide on p. 169 for how to start exercising, what to do and how to get the best out of it.

5

OFF I GO

It's the end of my first week. Full of early enthusiasm, I've had three training sessions and I'm feeling good. I've changed my diet, but the weight loss is minimal. This, I tell myself, is because Imran is busy changing my fat to muscle, and muscle weighs more than fat.

Soon, my change of diet is going to kick in and I'm going to see the pounds melting away.

Fat Bloke's Post-Life-Change Menu

❑ **5.30 a.m.** Have a cup of tea. If I'm training with Imran, I'll eat my breakfast now: a bowl of crunchy oat cereal with semi-skimmed milk and fresh fruit, and a banana. Then I'll head over to the gym, do my session and go into work.

❑ **7.30 a.m.** Breakfast. I'm now bringing healthy cereal into work with me, and I'll eat my cereal and fruit now if I haven't had a session with Imran. If I haven't trained, I'll try and get some exercise in – a run at the gym near work. When I get back, or if I arrive after a session with Imran, I'll have fresh fruit and yoghurt.

❏ **10.30 a.m.** Cup of tea.

❏ **1 p.m.** Lunch. As with breakfast, I'm bringing in more from home. If I can, I'll bring in leftovers from the previous night's supper. If I can't, I'll go to the canteen and have the lightest protein I can – fish is great – and skip any sauces. I'll have plain veg and salad, but only the lightest vinaigrette on the salad, no creamy dressing. I'll go for lots of fresh stuff, piling up tomatoes and cucumbers, as well as mixed bean salads. It looks like a lot and feels satisfying. Afterwards, I'll have fresh fruit and maybe some yoghurt. I'll drink plain water.

❏ **4 p.m.** Snack of fruit and nuts. I've started buying big bags from health-food stores and making up my own mix in a plastic box: prunes, figs, dates, apricots, mango (a big natural sugar hit here, as the sugar in dried fruit is very concentrated), brazil nuts, walnuts, hazelnuts and pumpkin seeds. All lovely, healthy stuff that provides masses of energy. I'll also eat some of this in the morning if I need an energy boost. I might add that it's very good for the bowels, keeping everything nice and regular …

❏ **8–9 p.m.** I have to admit that, when I get home,

I'm having a glass or two of wine, just to unwind and relax. Dinner is much the same as before but without the carbs, so no potatoes or pasta. Instead, meat or fish with lots of vegetables and salad, maybe another glass of wine, but no puddings.

Impressive, don't you think?

I do allow myself some slack, though. At weekends, I'll eat what the family is having, and I look forward to a lovely cheese and ham toasted panini on Saturday mornings with a large latte while my son does his dance classes. I don't think that can do too much harm.

I'm certainly pretty pleased. I've changed my diet, and I'm working out approximately 300 per cent more than usual. Surely the weight is about to fall off, any minute now …

Hmmm.

It's week two, and nothing much is happening. I'm chronicling my weight loss in an occasional column for the Health section in the *Daily Mail*. I've got an email address for readers to write to, and the messages are flooding in. Lots are very supportive, and it turns out that hundreds, if not thousands, of men are in the same condition as I am, and as keen as I am to do something about it. That makes me more determined than ever to stick to my new regime, and doubly convinced that I did the right thing sharing my struggle with others. It helps to know I'm not alone and encourages my efforts to know that people are following them.

It also means that I start to attract some interesting email correspondence. A lot of people out there are interested in weight loss, and quite a few have an absolutely fail-safe method for me to follow. They're keen for me to try their slimming pills (the magic herbal ones that mysteriously dissolve fat, just like that), or their slimming tea (two cups a day and your fat is magically gone), or their special methods (eat two steaks for every meal for three weeks and you will lose a stone, guaranteed – yeah, you might, I suppose, but come on! Does that sound like a sensible way to eat?). If there are any testimonials, it's always gush about how wonderful the method is, from someone called A.E. of Sheffield, or Mrs F. from Brighton and Hove, with no way of finding out who the hell they are, if they really exist and if they truly are satisfied in every way with their fat-eating tablets. Or the green tea, sold for some astronomical price, comes with some fine print – must be used in conjunction with a calorie-controlled diet. Oh, what a surprise! You mean drinking tea alone doesn't do shit? Knock me down with a feather, mate …

There are also some more sane-sounding messages from people who intrigue me: a hypnotherapist named

Maria tells me that she can alter my mental processes and help me lose weight.

I'm interested and file this email away just in case I turn out to need it.

But you don't get the smooth without the rough. Besides friendly, encouraging, polite emails, I also receive a few of the other sort. This one stands out:

> Hi Bruce,
>
> Stop kidding yourself, you won't reach retirement age.
>
> I'm nearly 70 and walk 6 miles a day, no wasting money on a gym.
>
> Give up the gym. In the time it takes you to drive there, change, work out, shower, dress and drive home, you could have walked 6 miles as well.
>
> Carry on drinking and you die early – switch to Diet Coke and forget your macho ego. Have wine only with a meal.
>
> You have always been FAT because of the calorie intake – NO EXCUSES.
>
> Best wishes, but I expect you to fail like most other obese people with NO CONTROL over their lives.
>
> Terry

Woah, that's straight talking! I feel a bit chilled by Terry's email, but it's also bracing. My whole problem is distilled down into one sentence: too many calories in the form of excess food and drink have made me fat. But Terry's certainty that I'm going to fail only makes me more determined to prove him wrong. Besides, I've tackled the eating problem, haven't I? My diet is much better, I know that. I feel better on it.

So why aren't I losing any weight?

6

MY FATAL FLAW

Just in case you hadn't noticed, I like a drink. I have fallen into a habit. It's the habit of drinking just about every night.

I have to think about this now, because it's been over two weeks. I'm training with the Bastard three times a week. Besides the boxing, the running and the cardio, there are crunches, press-ups, sit-ups. Imran is working me hard. When I show signs of slacking, he yells, 'Come on, you great lump of lard,' and urges me on, telling me not to quit, to hang on in there. When he's not abusing me, he's very supportive, telling me I'm doing well and praising my fitness levels. He also texts and phones me in between sessions to keep encouraging me. His dedication is really helping to keep me at it when, previously, I might have given up. And I can see results already: my eyes are brighter, my muscles feel tighter and I've got more energy. That's all great, and helps me carry on.

I've been on my new, healthier diet. Okay, I'm not

counting calories or anything, but I am thinking about what I eat and keeping an eye on everything I consume. I mean, I *know* what healthy food is. I *know* what unhealthy food is. So if I eat healthy food, I'm going to lose weight, right?

Wrong.

My weight loss is minimal. It's getting me down. Where am I going wrong?

Okay. The truth is, I know why it's not working. It's those glasses of delicious cold white wine in the evening after work that are scuppering everything. I realize that I haven't really made the mental shift I thought I had. In fact, I've secretly made a deal with myself not to change my life too much. I thought that if I increased my activity and cut down on bad foods, I could carry on doing the thing that has really contributed most to my weight gain over the years, and that's drinking.

From the early days in the music business, through to my time in Australia on the rigs and, later, in the world of acting, drinking is what I've done to have a good time. A glass of wine or beer has been my way to relax, become uninhibited, feel happier with myself and my lot. I've got used to rewarding myself at the end of a long day with the adult version of a bag of sweets: a drink. The fact that it also makes me feel cooler, more chilled and a touch hazy at the edges only adds to its appeal.

The first fortnight has passed and, as I'm standing on the scales feeling frustrated that, despite my efforts, I still can't see far enough over my manly girth to read the damn thing, *ping!*, I have a light-bulb moment.

Alcohol has to go.

My problem is a fairly simple one. I've got into a bad habit and the trigger for my bad habit is getting home from work and cooking a meal. I've got so used to pouring myself a glass of wine when I put my apron on and start slicing the onions that I don't even think about it. Then Tanya and I chat happily away about our respective days, sipping at our glasses without really noticing. It's not unusual for us to finish the bottle between us. We both think of it as a way to relax a little, as a reward at the end of a long, hard day. Lots of my friends are the same.

I think the problem is that I haven't realised what I'm doing. Now that I've woken up to the fact that I'm drinking every night, it will be easy to crack down on it. I decide that I'll only drink on Fridays and Saturdays and give it up on school nights. Easy.

My first week without booze is not what you'd call a resounding success. I drink every day *except* Monday.

The second week is a bit better. I don't drink on Sunday, Monday or Tuesday. I find that if I drink a big glass of sparkling water with a touch of lime cordial in it as soon as I get in from work, and then pour myself another to have with dinner, I can kill the Wine Demon.

It becomes a battle of the wills: me versus the bottle. If I can resist the call till after the start of dinner, I'm fine. But I can't always resist.

Have you ever noticed that, once you make a decision to quit something, even if you're not that bothered about it in the first place, you start to really want it? It's partly because I've decided that I'm not supposed to drink that I fail so spectacularly in my second week of trying to keep off the sauce. From Wednesday onwards, I hammer my liver, culminating in the mother of all BBQs, where I get well and truly trollied. I wake up the next morning resolving never to drink again because I feel like utter shit.

I'm disappointed in myself and I still haven't lost any weight.

I've written about my battle with the Wine Demon in my *Daily Mail* column. I've had quite a lot of feedback from my readers about how to get round my craving for a glass of wine in the evening. Charles suggests that I boil it up with a mulling spice bag (to make it taste nasty? Or to get rid of the alcohol? Either way, it sounds disgusting). Phil says that I simply shouldn't buy the stuff. Blindingly obvious, maybe, but also weirdly impossible. I don't live on my own in the house, after

—

all, and I do have guests and visitors from time to time.
I also get another missive from Terry:

> *Hi Bruce*
>
> *It's me again, TERRY.*
>
> *If you are struggling with the Wine Demon,
> stand up and make a decision. Don't be a WIMP.*
>
> *Drink wine only once or twice a week with a
> meal and NOT 3 bottles.*
>
> *I had a great American Football friend who
> had a car accident in the early 1960s after drink-
> ing, and he realized that he could have killed the
> love of his life.*
>
> *HE NEVER DRANK AGAIN.*
>
> *We used to go into bars in Chicago and order
> 2 DIET COKES. It's EASY, stand up and take
> control of your life and forget the macho, ego crap.*
>
> *Talk to you soon*
>
> *Terry*

As before, I feel a bit miffed when I get this email.
What's he talking about – macho, ego crap? I don't see
the issue as being about my massive ego, and I certainly
don't think that hard drinking makes me manly (after
all, I'm a civilised-glass-of-wine man, not a fifteen-pints-
and-watch-me-spew bloke). I just like a drink of an
evening. But something in his message is ringing true.

It's about taking control, making decisions and sticking to them. Remember that saying: the spirit is willing but the flesh is weak? Well, it's about making yourself conquer that weakness and stay completely strong.

I remind myself that no one is forcing me to drink a drop. Every mouthful I take is a choice made by me. And, once I let myself take that first sip, I know damn well I'm going to take another and then another, fill up my glass when it's empty and probably sink three-quarters of a bottle before I'm done. I know this – and yet I can't seem to stop myself. How do I cope with wanting it?

This isn't the first addiction I've tackled. When I gave up smoking three years ago, I was on between twenty and forty cigarettes a day, and I'd been a proper smoker since I was fourteen. I was completely dedicated to it, it was a cup of a coffee and a cigarette first thing in the morning, and on I went for the entire day, really hitting the cigs when I started drinking in the evening. I had one attempt at giving up, but the stress of my father-in-law's death and the cravings I experienced meant that I caved in. Then, in January 2006, I said to Tanya, 'I'm going to stop smoking, for good.' I knew I was in a bad way because of the fags. I couldn't run, I couldn't breathe properly, I was sweating all the time and, crucially, I wasn't enjoying it. The only fag I liked was the first one – the rest were just feeding the craving. Then there was the expense, the smell and the fact that my kids were growing up with smokers for parents. All of it added up to one thing: I had to stop.

The wife and I gave up at the same time, and I haven't smoked since. It was pure will power. I made a decision – 'I'm never going to smoke another cigarette' – and I knew that meant I couldn't touch another. Ever.

I've never regretted it. Of course, there's no one so bad as a reformed smoker – I can't stand cigarettes now. I hate the smell of smoke on other people, on their clothes or breath, and I ask people not to smoke near me. It seems as though, with me, it's all or nothing.

So I know I've got the strength to force myself to change, because I've already done it, but only when I choose to use it, and the problem is that, when you are close up to yourself and your own behaviour, you sometimes can't see your own destructive patterns – or you choose not to see them. But I know enough to realize that, once you've accepted that you're doing bad things to yourself that make you miserable in the long run (even if it feels as though they're making you happy) and that you need to change in order to be happier in the long term – well, that's the key.

And Terry has just put it in a nutshell. It's EASY. As long as you stand up and take control.

As I struggle on, I'm feeling increasingly depressed and worried. Why is it so difficult to deny myself a drink?

I'm finding it almost as difficult as I did when I gave up smoking. Does this mean I'm an alcoholic?

I can't seem to regulate my intake or the quantity. The little Wine Demon just climbs on to my shoulder and urges me on, and I can't help myself.

This is a massive thing for me, as I think it is for the nation as a whole. Is there something in the British psyche that can't stop itself getting drunk?

I discuss my worries with Tanya, and she says that, since her father died, I've been drinking to medicate myself against the grief and stress; now it's become a habit I really do need to break. She doesn't think I'm an alcoholic – not yet, at least. I just need to get my head into the right place, and I'll be able to do it.

But Tanya has got amazing will power. She tells me that she's not going to have a drink from now until her sister's wedding, and I know she'll do it. She gives me a handy tip – to spend ten minutes a day visualizing all the bad effects that result from alcohol, not just weight gain but liver damage, cancer risk, not to speak of horrible hangovers and the embarrassing things you do and say under the influence. I guess I'm lucky, having a beautiful psychologist wife on hand whenever I need her …

I take my kids to London's International Music Fair. My daughter is severely disappointed when she realizes that it is a trade fair and not a series of concerts, but I have a great time. Then I see a great bass-guitar hero of mine from one of the greatest prog-rock bands of the seventies. I've not seen him close up since Rotterdam 1977. I'm shocked at his appearance. Okay, he's older – we all are – but he looked pasty, bloated and downright ill from too much booze throughout his lifetime. You can see the effects all over him, and they're not pretty. He doesn't look like he's feeling too chipper either. I know for sure I don't want to look that way, and my one-time-hero is a walking advertisement for cutting down.

So, that night, I go home and sink nearly a whole bottle of wine by myself.

Christ, what is my problem??? Why can't I do this?

I feel so disappointed with myself (and so terrible the following morning) that for the next few days, I stay off the booze completely, fighting the urge to drink in the evening with those big glasses of sparkling water and lime cordial. Immediately, I feel better – clearer-headed, brighter-eyed, more focused and with more energy.

To my huge delight, some weight starts to come off at last.

Just in case I slip up again, I book an appointment with the hypnotherapist who contacted me. It's time to get some more help, and I'm going to ask for my weakness with the booze to be taken into consideration, Your Honour.

7

RELAX, RELAX ...

So it's just over a month since it all began and, believe it or not, Fat Bloke *is* slimming.

Yes, in four weeks I've dropped approximately five pounds and my waist is narrower by a whole inch! I'm 15 stone 7lb.

I feel elated. Seeing the results of my efforts is really encouraging, and I'm full of enthusiasm again. But there's no doubt that cutting down on the booze is what's done it. Somehow I had managed to miss the fact that I was sabotaging the whole diet by drinking. After all, what is alcohol but sugar? Would I go home and pour a bag of Tate & Lyle down my throat? Of course not. But that's the equivalent of what I was doing.

I'm not one to obsess over calories, and nor are any of the blokes I know, but it doesn't take a genius to realize that wine is stuffed with them. There are about a hundred calories in a medium-sized glass of white wine alone. A few of those, and I'm drinking the equivalent of another whole meal every day but without any of the benefits of food (such as nutrition). And a hangover needs feeding with lots of sugar and fat, or at least mine do. No wonder I wasn't losing any weight.

So what's the secret?

We all know that the only way to lose weight is to expend more energy than you consume, so there's no doubt that Imran is a big factor. I'm still turning up at the gym in my shabby old gear (I've made a deal with myself that I will not buy any more until my current kit fits me the way it used to, i.e. comfortably rather than tightly strained in places), and I've learned that personal trainers aren't born, they're constructed from steel and programmed with software the military can only dream about. The Bastard, as I still call him (but only mentally of course, as he's a hell of a lot stronger than me), makes me sprint the length of the room, do ten squat jumps, sprint back to him and do twenty jab/cross uppercuts and hooks as I run and do the whole thing all over again. And don't get me started on the sit-ups. I might be tired and out of breath at the end, but the amazing thing is, I can do it.

And the great plus about working out in a gym is that everyone is in the same boat – sweaty, knackered and couldn't care less what the next guy is doing because they're concentrating on trying not to keel over.

In four weeks I am transformed: I have better stamina and fitness than in years, and I look younger and fitter, more like forty than seventy, as I did previously. I may not have lost shedloads of weight, but I always knew it would take time. My metabolism is slower than it used to be, for one thing. But I want to lose the weight at a sensible, sustainable rate, so that I keep it off. Five pounds in four weeks is great, as far as I'm concerned. It's nearly half a stone in just a month – that's no time at all. And I mean to make sure it stays off too.

Even though I regard myself as open-minded, I must admit to being a bit sceptical when it comes to hypnosis. I don't like the idea of giving a stranger power over me and interfering with my free will – assuming it works at all, which I'm dubious about. But Maria's email interested me. She offered me 'hypnotic stomach stapling' – she would be able to remove the desire to overeat with a few simple hypnosis sessions in tandem with acupuncture. Although I don't feel that I am overeating now I'm on my new diet, every little helps. And I might mention my real struggle of giving up the nightly tipple and see if she can do anything to alter my mindset. It would be great just to be able to say no and not even think about it.

So I take Maria up on her offer and make an appointment at her room in Harley Street. When I get there, Maria is very personable and eager to please, although she seems a bit nervous, which is perhaps because she knows our meeting might appear in a national newspaper. That said, she tries very hard to put me at my ease and sets out her stall, so to speak, by giving me a brief rundown of what she is about, the treatment I'm about to receive. Then she takes some of my medical history.

Once that is done, it's down to business.

I've had acupuncture before, and I'm fine with it, but if you haven't, the idea of it can be daunting. How can those sharp needles not hurt when they go into the skin? Well, weirdly, they don't, if your practitioner is experienced and gentle, and Maria is both. I know I'm in good hands, and I don't feel any pain, just a slight pinch as each needle goes in.

Maria concentrates on the ear (which apparently, in some acupuncture circles, is described as an inverted foetus – check it out, I can see it), inserting four or five needles in each. Once they are all in, I lie back on Maria's couch and the hypnosis begins. Maria sits down in a chair next to me, tells me to relax and breathe deeply, and begins to speak very softly.

After this point, I'm in a strange half-sleeping, half-waking state where I have snatches of feeling aware of what's going on. I can hear Maria talking, but I keep forgetting where I am and feel instead as if I'm dream-ing. When I hear her voice, I wonder who on earth is talking away and why. When I remember what's going on, I try and catch up with the session, but it always eludes me.

When the session ends, Maria wakes me, or brings me back, or however you want to describe it. I feel ... well, normal, but a nice normal: refreshed, positive, quite cheerful.

'I've planted seeds in your mind,' Maria tells me. 'You won't be aware of them. You won't even know when they're triggered. But you'll feel more in control of your weight and your eating. The whole thing will be easier now. You'll want to eat less because you'll be able to visualize your body and want to change it.'

I feel very glad about that, and somehow sure that what she says is true. Then I mention the demon drink. Maria nods wisely and tells me that she has dropped a seed in my mind about alcohol too, and soon I'll start to see my drinking decrease.

I feel a little sceptical about that, but I'm keen to be proved wrong, so I try and stay positive.

Maria teaches me a technique to use if I find myself feeling stressed or tempted to throw all my good resolutions to the wind. I have to make a circle with the thumb and forefinger of my left hand, press hard and take three deep breaths in and out, filling the lungs completely, nice and slow, then release my fingers.

'That will recharge the effects of the session,' Maria says. Then she removes the acupuncture pins from my ears and inserts one tiny needle on a sticky backing in each ear to wear until the next session. 'These will help to keep your kidneys and liver in balance. They'll improve your overall health and the flow of energy through your body.'

I don't know much about eastern theories of energy flow and so on, but I'm willing to believe there's something in them, so I'm happy to wear my little ear needles for as long as it takes. That evening I promptly lose one after a shower but, when I email Maria, she writes back to say she'll send more with instructions about how to put them in.

Back at home, I wait for something magical to happen but, of course, it doesn't. I eat my dinner as usual, and have a drink as usual, though only one, and go to bed. But I can't help feeling that whatever Maria's done is probably buried so deeply, I'm not even aware of it. And I have the strange feeling that it is going to help me …

My next weigh-in sees me drop another pound, and then I lose another after that. I'm down to 15 stone 5lb.

Six weeks in, and I'm losing a pound a week. It might not be the greatest weight loss ever, but it's fine for me. I've always known that I want to take it slowly. Crash diets are bound to fail, we all know that.

Imran reminds me that all my activity means that

some of my fat is being converted to muscle, which weighs more than fat. I used to be a fit and muscly twenty-something when I worked on the rigs, and that muscle can be pumped up again fairly fast as soon as I start using it, and that, ironically, will make me heavier. It could be another explanation for my failure to lose weight at first. He tells me to keep an eye on my measurements and how my clothes are fitting rather than obsessing over my weight.

This seems like sensible advice, although it leaves me a bit confused. According to the Body Mass Index chart, the heavier you are, the more overweight you are. But muscle-men are the heaviest of all. Are they chronically obese? I decide to investigate this a bit more at some point, because it doesn't seem to make sense.

But, in the meantime, I've reduced my blubber footprint by half a stone. That's pretty good in my book.

Lots of people are writing to me, offering me lots of free tuition, massage, advice, magic pills, you name it. I suppose that is one of the perks of being able to use my celebrity. Because I've got a well-known face from the telly, I can get a column in the *Daily Mail*. Then people want to give me things for free. Okay for you, Fat Bloke, I hear you say (and not for the first time), but the rest of us don't have people lining up to give us free treatment. That's true, and it's not fair, but let me put it this way: I'm doing all this so you don't have to if it turns out to be a waste of time. And, believe me, not all the attention I get is of the pleasant kind.

I must admit to being quite perplexed when it comes to celebrity culture. I know I'm classed by some people as a 'celeb' and obviously I have a face people recognize. Millions of people watch *The Bill* and after five years, I can hardly be surprised that some of the people who watch it feel they know me or are interested in what I do. Perhaps I'm naïve, but I don't think of myself as a celebrity. I just happen to be someone who is fortunate enough to be doing a job that I love with a passion. Being well known as a result is, to be honest, a part of the job I could quite happily not have in my life. But it's there, and I live with it and, in the main, people are kind, generous with their words and supportive. I say in the main because, within that hugely supportive community, there is a minority whose role, it seems, is to knock those who are living their dream. I could speculate on their motivation, but I won't.

It's just after my third column in the *Daily Mail* has been published. It's a pretty innocuous bit of fun directed at my trainer, Imran, and letting the readers know how I'm getting on weight-wise and with my battle against drinking wine every night.

I'm just coming out of the tube station when my phone beeps to announce a new message in my Fat

Bloke inbox. So I open it. Almost without exception, emails from my readers have been friendly and encouraging, often full of advice. But this one reads:

> *Pig ignorant or is it ignorant pig? Have a coronary you walking obesity.*

I feel sick and chilled, stunned by the incredible hate behind such a message. Somehow, one nasty, anonymous little spew of hate can undo all the good that those other positive, encouraging emails offer. I should be used to this by now – having a well-known face doesn't always bring me welcome attention. I've had my fair share of abuse shouted at me in the streets, or someone approaching me with unexplained anger written all over their face to ask me who the hell I think I am, but that's very rare.

The worst of it is that it stirs up depressing, unhappy memories. When I was the fat child all those years ago I was badly bullied, and I guess the playground is never far away. At seven years old, I was different – I weighed twelve stone, for a start – and so the bullies came out of the woodwork, as they do, and proceeded to humiliate and terrify me in equal measure. I distinctly remember being in a sort of hide that had been created by some kids out of a heap of council lumber left by the side of the road for a future job, and there I was, happily munching on something or other, when some older kids came by, looked in and announced to one and all that there was a fat kid in there. So they proceeded to take my food, rough me up and go on their way.

This horrible little email reminds me of all that: the fear and pain and self-loathing. But I decide to turn it into something positive: I'm going to take all that bad feeling and make it work for me. Hanging on to my weight is hanging on to garbage from the past. It's the result of behaviour I learnt forty years ago. I have to break habits, get past it, learn new ways of coping with things and not turn to food and drink for comfort or support or when I feel low.

I'm half a stone lighter, I remind myself. And that's how I'm going to stay.

Then, just to cheer me up, I get a message that makes me smile:

Hi Bruce,

I was very interested to hear about your weight battle. Yes, I'm yet another of your twin brothers! Virtually interchangeable statistics, weight issues (and looks).

I'm a gay man, and if it helps (it may not …) I think you are very handsome and, with some weight loss, you could become a real gay pin-up, à la Ross Kemp.

Hope this won't make you head straight for the
pizzas, chocolate and wine!
Best of luck, mate
Adrian.

The sympathy, kindness and gentle flattery make me feel a great deal better and wipe out the effects of the earlier message. And, let's face it, if the prospect of being a gay icon doesn't spur me on to succeed – well, nothing will!

A few days later I decide to see how the old body is responding to the weight loss and see if I've moved anywhere on the near-death scale. The British Heart Foundation did me proud when I went to them at the start of all this. Now I decide to go to a company called Cardio Direct, a London-based outfit that specializes in cardiovascular tests for both the individual and the corporate sector. Obviously, this one costs, but I think it's worth getting an in-depth overhaul, so I go for it and book an appointment.

It's six weeks in and my weight loss is steady if slow, averaging out at around a pound a week. I don't know why it's not falling off me: I'm sticking to my diet resolutions, and I'm still exercising. Perhaps it's because I'm still drinking, but I know for certain that I'm not drinking as much as I was. Surely my diet has room for a glass of wine of an evening? Can that really be making the difference?

Anyway, I'm sure that since I saw Maria the hypnotherapist, my drinking is gradually decreasing so I make an appointment with her. I have another session with Maria, just like the first: a warm, relaxing hour that I can barely remember afterwards.

Then I trot down Harley Street to Cardio Direct for my thorough check-up.

I'm certainly put through my paces. There is a lead ECG (or electrocardiogram, to give its full name – basically, an electrical heart test), which records the rhythm and electrical activity of my heart, picking up any abnormalities related to fast or slow heartbeats, high blood pressure and heart muscle disease.

Then there is an exercise ECG. I pound away on a treadmill while the machine reads how my heart responds to physical stress.

The very friendly consultants record my family history (which is not great – there are plenty of heart attacks and strokes), take a body composition (height, weight, Body Mass Index, waist-hip ratio, etc.), take blood tests, do a blood-pressure profile and urine tests, monitor respiratory function and, last, but not least, do a lifestyle review (my diet, physical activity and so on).

'We'll send your full report to you by post,' says the

consultant, 'but, in the meantime, I can say that you're very fit.'

Excellent. This is good news. I know for sure that it's my exercise regime that's getting me these good results. I'm looking forward to finding out the fuller picture in due course.

I feel like I've got all the bases covered: I'm making all the changes I can; I have a trainer, a hypnotherapist, a full body MOT ...

What more can I do?

'I'm proud of you,' says Tanya. 'You're doing really well.'

That certainly helps.

8

SPLAT!!!

My results are back from Cardio Direct. The upshot is that the results are all encouraging, with no damage to my heart, good blood pressure, and my kidneys are okay. There are some concerns with my Body Mass Index – it's 31.7 rather than a perfect 20–25, but it's still down from my original 34 when I started all this over two months ago.

The report concludes that I'm in a low-risk group for future cardio events. In other words, there's no immediate worry that I'm going to have a heart attack. This is great news. But they stress that I need to lower my weight. Preaching to the converted there, guys. I'm already doing my best. But the report helps me reinvigorate my enthusiasm.

After all, my target is still daunting:

START WEIGHT:	15 stone 12lb
TARGET WEIGHT:	12 stone 12lb
TOTAL TO LOSE:	3 stone, or 42lb
WEIGHT LOST SO FAR:	9lb in 9 weeks
STILL TO GO:	33lb in 24 weeks, or almost 1.5lb a week.

It's mid July, and I've want to lose this weight by next January. It doesn't seem long at all. I'm beginning to realize that I'll have to take this seriously if I'm going to achieve my goal. I've got to double my weekly weight loss.

I decide to invest in some CDs that will help me lose weight. Apparently the key to changing a lot of our behaviour is in something called neuro-linguistic programming. If I've understood it correctly, it means using new language and new mental techniques to help you see your behaviour in a new light. I've realized already that it's hard to stand back and view my own behaviour objectively, so I think that anything that helps in that direction must be worth investigating. I was very sceptical at first about the mind-training stuff, but I'm beginning to realize that losing weight is all about mind over matter. My biggest challenge in losing weight is me. How can I simultaneously want to lose weight and also scupper all my efforts by eating and drinking too much when I *know* those things will stop me losing weight?

I don't know, and perhaps if I had iron self-discipline, it wouldn't be a problem but, like most people, I'm not always rigidly strong, and I've got a lifetime of bad eating habits and a challenging relationship with food to tackle.

At first, I thought I could do this entirely alone with one or two easy lifestyle changes – a bit less of this and that, and a bit more exercise. Now I understand that I'm going to need help to see this through. If I really am going to lose those pounds, I'm going to have get strength and determination from wherever I find it and, if that's a hypnotherapist or mind-programming CDs, so be it.

I buy the weight-loss CDs by Paul McKenna and put them on my iPod. I listen to them quite often, because they're wonderfully relaxing. Sometimes I get on the tube, switch on, close my eyes and relax. A soothing voice begins talking to me over a background of swirly music. Sometimes the voice is double or even triple tracked as it talks on, each track saying something different, calm, serene and reassuring. It's so relaxing and seems to sink so deeply into my consciousness that I can hardly remember what the voice says when I stop listening.

One thing the tape asks me is to imagine the size I want to be, and I can see myself, slim and trim in a great suit, and I remember why I really want to succeed at this.

The CD doesn't claim to work alone: I already have to have made the decision to lose weight and the lifestyle changes to allow that to happen. Instead, it works on underlining and reinforcing that decision.

Personally, I find it really helpful. It keeps me focused on the positive nature of what I'm doing.

Something's working, anyway.

Fifteen stone is in sight, and I like the look of it.

I think that the only way to get on top of this weight-loss thing is to be in a good routine: a routine of exercise and good diet where you manage to cover all the problem areas by planning ahead.

That's how I've coped so far and I've got a good lot of weight loss to show for it.

❑ I have my training sessions booked, and I have to say that paying for your exercise is a great motivator. I haven't once cried off.

❑ I'm in a good place at home: the right kinds of food are in the cupboards and I'm cooking and eating the kind of food that's going to help me lose weight.

❑ I've got my eating-at-work sorted too, with the help of packed lunches and making good choices when I do eat in the canteen.

❑ Yes, I'm still drinking a bit, probably a bit more than I should, but I think Maria's hypnotherapy is helping me cut down.

But take me out of this comfort zone and everything goes horribly wrong …

It starts off with a trip to Leipzig in Germany to film a collaboration between *The Bill* and *Soko Leipzig*, a German cop-show. At first, I'm worried about how I will cope with eating when I'm less in control, as all my meals will be in the hotel or on set, so no home cooking for me. But it turns out I needn't have worried – the hotel food is good. Breakfast is the same as it is in hotels across the world: a good mix of fresh fruit, cereals and yoghurts, along with all the Continental stuff – the croissants, the Danish pastries and so on. This being Germany, there is also a selection of heavy black breads, cheeses and hams, which are normal breakfast foods over there. So it's easy to make my usual choices, and great to be able to take advantage of the pool on site. I love swimming, and it's excellent exercise. I start off with early nights and getting up at 6 a.m. for a swim before work.

On set, the food is not that different from the stuff we have on *The Bill* set in Wimbledon, except that it is generally better, with an excellent choice of meat and fish dishes, with plenty of veg and salad. As long as I avoid the creamy sauces, the bread and the pasta/potato axis, I'm sure I'm making healthy choices.

My worry is the evenings. When you're in a foreign country, with no intelligible telly to watch, and out of your zone, it's easy to hear the call of the bar. After a hard day's work, it's only natural to want to kick back, and the general sense of being away from home can mean that it can feel like a bit of a party. Luckily, I fight that feeling and only have a couple of beers over the whole of the week I'm in Germany. I'm still in healthy-eating mode.

Then it's off to France for a week's holiday, which will culminate in my sister-in-law's wedding.

And this is where I come badly unstuck …

Being in France, the land of gourmet eating, with my family and a great party atmosphere, means that all the rules seem to go out of the window. Do you ever feel that? You're usually good but, when you're away from home and off the leash, you go for it. That's me.

Not only am I in the land of food, I'm also in the land of wine. Literally. We're staying right in one of the oldest vineyards in St Emilion, one of the most famous wine-producing regions in France. They're making the stuff right outside my window.

Well, what would you do?

Let's just say it all goes to hell in a handcart.

We're staying in a rented house. There's a big party of us: six adults and two kids. As soon as I arrive in our house, I feel my mindset change. We're on holiday! We're in France, the home of fine cuisine and excellent wine! I'm going to enjoy myself and put my diet and weight out of my mind.

There are lots of social engagements and people to visit in the run-up to the wedding. Wherever we go, we're offered delicious food and plenty of beer and wine. I take whatever I'm offered because, what the hell, I'm on holiday, right? I'm not going to come all the way to France and start saying no to everything.

To be fair, at first I do try to be moderate. But St Emilion is in the south-west of France, and the gastronomic specialities are not exactly lightweight. Here, all the restaurants offer duck, foie gras and truffles. The food is rich and often comes drenched in creamy, buttery sauces. Delicious ... The vegetables are wonderful too – good, honest local produce. I decide that I'm not going to pig out exactly, and I'll make the better, plainer choice where I can, but I'm not going to abstain either. I love good food enough to want to try some of the fantastic dishes offered to us.

I don't even realize that my alcohol intake is doubling, if not tripling. We're drinking with every meal except breakfast. At lunch, we'll open a bottle of wine or two, and lunch might end up drifting into dinner without me even noticing. Or we'll have a couple of glasses with lunch and then go out for a great meal that isn't complete without some of the excellent local wines. In fact, we're eating out most nights.

It's not that I'm getting hammered every night. It's just that I'm drinking every day.

Then comes the wedding and, I have to be honest – I do let rip. It's a big party and I intend to join in. I've been very good for weeks on end now, and it feels great to cast caution to the winds and let my hair down. It's just the once, after all. As soon as I get back home, I intend to go straight back to my disciplined habits.

Wow, what a party. We all have a great time and give my sister-in-law a memorable send-off into her married life.

Then it's back to Leipzig for another week's filming.

The strange thing is, it's not the same as it was in my first week at all. I do try and cut back on the rich food, as I'm definitely feeling that I've over-indulged. In fact, I'm quite good about that. It doesn't seem so hard to go back to my sensible eating routine. What's changed is the drinking. Whereas before I had a couple of beers over the course of an entire week, now I'm drinking every night.

I've got back into that old habit again. My week in France has undone all the good work I'd put in to retraining myself. Now it's hard not to open a bottle of wine as soon as the working day is over. The easiest thing, it turns out, is falling off the wagon.

When I get back home, I'm feeling bloated, and the mirror tells me I'm looking bloated too. I get on the scales.

HOLY SHIT!!! I've put on six pounds! My weight has rocketed back up to 15 stone 6lb. Weeks of hard work wasted.

I'm really disappointed with myself, as well as horrified that I've been able to put on weight so quickly. It's brought it home to me how much what I put into my body affects me.

I feel as though this is a make or break moment. What am I going to do? Am I going to give this all up as a gruelling race I can never win or get to the end of and go back to closing my mind and my eyes to my health and appearance?

Or am I going to put it behind me and start work to lose those pounds all over again?

9

THE CROSSROADS

It's the end of July, and I've put back on six, hard-worked-off pounds. I've wiped out half of my achievement.

But it's all not all bad news. I'm determined to stick with my weight loss. Once, I'd have felt extremely depressed and guilty about this, and probably given up the new regime. This time, I'm eager to get back on the wagon. I had a great time and a complete blow-out. But now it's over.

Yes, I wish I hadn't put back on quite so much weight. But this is supposed to be a realistic way of losing weight, and the reality is that occasionally I'm going to be going to a wedding or a party, or Christmas or a birthday will come along and I'm going to make the most of it.

I'm also going to find it easier now that I'm back home and back into the routine and the swing of things. It makes me realize how much of our lives is habit, and how much what we eat is simply what we've trained ourselves to eat.

Right, so I'm going to have to be tough on myself now and go back to my good-eating plan.

A typical day goes like this:

Breakfast:	Oat cereal, skimmed milk, fruit and yoghurt
Lunch:	Some lightly cooked fish with a big plateful of salad
	Fruit salad with Greek yoghurt
	Lots of water
Snack:	Dried fruit and nuts
Dinner:	Meat or fish with lots of vegetables
	More fresh fruit
	One glass of wine, maybe two

I've come down hard on some of my weekend indulgences too. Now, I'm eating the light version of our Sunday lunch, cutting out the fatty bits, and I've decided to say goodbye to ham and cheese toasted paninis as well. And, if I order a latte, it's going to be a small one with skimmed milk. I'm really going to have to cut out my little treats if I'm going to get back on course.

By putting that weight back on, I've made life a lot harder for myself.

But at the same time as I'm telling myself that I'm going to be good from now on, there's an added complication. We're going on our family holiday next week. The wedding was not actually our annual break, just a very pleasant extra, thanks to my sister-in-law getting married in France. I've had this trip booked for ages, and I'm really looking forward to it. I've got three weeks off work – and, believe me, that much time off doesn't happen often. I've booked an apartment on the coast in Turkey in the beautiful seaside town of Foca (sounds like 'poacher') for me, Tanya and the kids to enjoy some quality time together. Come September, the kids'll be back at school and Tanya and I will be back into our hectic working schedules. We really need some down time together, and two weeks in the sun is absolutely the best way to get it.

But I'm also worried. I've just seen what the effects of time away from home can do to me. I'm carrying six pounds of blubber and, here I am, about to waltz off on holiday again. Am I really going to diet and watch my food and drink intake when I'm supposed to be enjoying myself? Come on!

My latest column in the *Daily Mail* details how I've fallen off the wagon and put some weight back on again. I try and put a brave face on it and announce that I'm reintroducing the strict regime with immediate effect and that I'm really not that depressed that I've put on weight. But the statistics at the end make gloomy reading:

Starting weight: 15 stone 12lb. After 10 weeks: 15 stone 6lb.

When I see it there in black and white, I feel bad

again. Six pounds in ten weeks! It sounds pretty poor. And I'm not the only one who thinks so.

> *Hi Bruce,*
>
> *Will you get a grip and stop whingeing?*
>
> *6lb lost in 10 weeks is abysmal – I've lost more than that in coin of the realm.*
>
> *After 10 weeks you should have dropped 20lb at least. I hope you have got rid of the personal trainer (rip-off merchants). You would be far better walking to the gym, don't go in, just turn around and walk home again. Better exercise and better value for money.*
>
> *What excuse are you going to use next time you fall off the wagon? Somebody's wedding, funeral or simply your football team winning?*
>
> *If you followed my regime you WOULD succeed but anything you do is down to YOU, nobody else. So just get on with it.*
>
> *Talk to you soon*
>
> *Your mate Terry*

Thanks, Tezza, mate!

But I know he's right, that's the killer. I can talk a good game – I can explain to myself exactly why six pounds overall is an excellent weight loss and explain with barrister-like brilliance how I lost almost a stone but then was forced to put half of it back on again because going to weddings and going away are, obviously, exceptional circumstances.

But, the truth is, I know that I haven't done very well, and I'm disappointed. I'm supposed to lose three stone by January. I've been losing weight for three months, I've got six months left and two and a half stone to go. Despite all my lifestyle changes, something isn't working.

And now I'm going on holiday again …

I suppose Terry's words must have had some kind of effect, or the stern talking to I gave myself has worked, because, as soon as we arrive in Turkey, I feel good.

The week we spent in France was about idleness and indulgence. We did almost nothing and ate vast quantities of rich food and drank buckets of wine.

This is different. The apartment is gorgeous, with a view over the Aegean sea. We're in a kind of hotel complex, so we can order food to be delivered to our room if we don't feel like cooking – and we don't. There's too much to do and see. The weather is amazing, and the heat acts as an appetite suppressant. As for alcohol – well, for most the day, it's water I crave, and cool juices. The food is about as healthy as you could ask for and basically encompasses my favourite kind of eating: lightly grilled fish or meat with masses of fresh vegetables and salads, and lots of fruit.

Hey, this is the holiday for me. And – it turns out – for my weight as well.

In France, I let go of all constraints. Here, I try to strike a balance. I make sure I get some exercise in by swimming twice, or even three or four times, a day, in the sea or in the hotel pool. I eat plenty, don't worry about that, but I can relax knowing that just about every-thing put in front of me is healthy: no creamy sauces, no plates of cheese, no fat-laden pâtés and puddings.

My alcohol consumption is also a lot lower than it was. Sometimes I have a beer with lunch, but the heat is so dehydrating that I prefer good, cold water. In the evening I have a glass of chilled rosé as the sun goes down. Once or twice, the missus and I get a taste for the wine and polish off a bottle between us. But, on three or four days, I don't drink at all. There's no special reason as such, I just don't fancy it.

I feel good while I'm on holiday. It feels as though I'm flushing out a lot of the bad stuff I've been filling my body with. Every time I go swimming, I get out feeling fresher and fitter. We're all tanning a bit in the hot sun, and it's giving us a healthy glow. This really is perfect R & R as far as I'm concerned.

I also enjoy it because I know that, with my daugh-ter on the cusp of being a teenager, there might not be too many idyllic family holidays left. She's still a kid right now, but soon she's going to be an independent spirit who can think of a million better things to do than hang out with her mum and dad, so I'm determined to make the most of this break.

When I get back from Turkey, I'm delighted to find that I've actually lost weight while on holiday. To be specific, I've lost four pounds! What a result. Perhaps I ought to move to the Mediterranean – it obviously suits me.

I'm delighted that I've managed to undo some of the damage and feel reinvigorated. And I've learned an important lesson: if you're trying to lose weight, there are no holidays or special occasions. For me, those will come (in moderation) when I've reached the weight I want to be. Until then, I can't afford to stop being vigilant, or I'll end up yo-yo-ing, then losing enthusiasm and giving up.

Another thing I've realized is that, deep down, I haven't been seeing eating and living healthily as being compatible with having a good time. Despite everything I've told myself, somewhere in my consciousness I've equated my new, weight-conscious lifestyle as being about denial. That's why I fell off the wagon so spectacularly in France, saying to myself: sod it, no denial now! Just complete indulgence!

The truth is, all that so-called indulgence had one effect, which was to make me feel terrible. There were pounding hangovers, raging thirsts, food cravings and a general sense that I was being an idiot but not being able to stop myself.

My holiday in Turkey has taught me that I can have a brilliant time and feel completely spoiled at the same time as being good to my body. In France, I forgot for a while that I am overweight and trying to shed my excess, and that is something I need to consider every single day until I succeed. In Turkey, I got myself focused again.

I'm 15 stone 2lb. Fitter, browner and happier.

10

ADVICE

I'm absolutely amazed by the number of diets out there.

We've all heard of the famous ones: Rosemary Conley's hip and thigh (low calorie and low fat), Atkins (low carbohydrate, high protein), GI (slow-energy-release foods), Weight Watchers (essentially a low-calorie diet, which, you may remember, I have first-hand experience of), Slimmer's World (a kind of food-combining, where proteins and carbs are eaten on alternate days – if I've understood it right!) and many, many more.

And it's not just the diets you can buy, but theories of diets and weight loss.

My inbox is packed with emails from people of all types – your average punters through to doctors of nutrition. They all have something they are keen to share with me: the no-nonsense, obvious path to weight loss. But the problem is, there are so many differing opinions …

If it isn't about the evils of fat, it's about the evils of carbohydrates.

If it isn't about eating little and often, it's about eating three solid meals with no snacks in between. Or it's about eating four small meals two and a half hours apart, and stopping food altogether at 6 p.m.

If it isn't about 'forget the diet, it's all in the exercise,' it's 'forget exercise, you can lose weight by eating to this simple plan' …

If it isn't about eating right for your blood type, it's about low GI, or protein-only, or carb curfews. Or only carbs one day, and only protein the next. Or keeping stress low. Or keeping it high. Who the hell knows?

Japanese diet? Or Mediterranean? Low fat or high fat? Count calories or don't count the damn things?

I'm so confused. I thought I knew the basics about weight loss, but it all sounds so bloody complicated. And there are plenty of people out there who will tell you earnestly and sincerely that you are going about it absolutely the wrong way. Even if I discount the people trying to sell me diet pills, slimming teas or other dubious aids, I've got hundreds swearing that their way is the best, most satisfying, most scientific way to lose weight.

What's happened to the western world? Why are there so many people who need to lose their fat?

I can't believe this is all about eating. I think we've got completely mixed up with our relationship to food somewhere along the line. Perhaps it's because we've been spoiled for far too long: there's been too much food, too much cheap rubbish designed to appeal to our sweet-toothed, fat-loving appetites. 'Do you want more?' the food industry asks us. 'Have more! Have it super-size! Have two for the price of one! Don't deny yourself – treat yourself. Don't bother cooking, we'll do that for you! It's as good as if you'd cooked it yourself, honestly …'

It's a con – and we have to share the blame, for giving in to all that. I mean, we know in our hearts that drinking a litre of coke with a meal can't be good for us, right? But lots of us still take the big option. We know that the food industry is out to make money from us and that our health is not its primary concern. But we still believe the pictures on the packet, even though we can see and taste that the reality is different.

The way things are going, that might have to change. There are world food shortages. The price of our basic food – flour, meat, dairy – is escalating. The cost of our basic foodstuffs has gone up 12.2 per cent in the last year and, for some products, it is much more than that. Bad weather means bad harvests, means less food. That's why the price of flour has risen all over the world, causing food riots in some countries.

Maybe our overeating isn't going to be a problem for much longer, because it's quite possible that those food shortages are going to have a real effect on our ability to buy food. And, if that happens, perhaps we'll see something similar to a return to wartime austerity.

This thought interests me, and I do a little research on the internet. I find out that, at the start of the Second World War, the UK imported a huge amount of food every year, around 70 per cent of the total, including more than 50 per cent of its meat, 70 per cent of its cheese and sugar, nearly 80 per cent of fruits and about 90 per cent of cereals and fats. As soon as war broke out, Britain's enemies laid siege to this country, preventing many of those imports from reaching us.

That meant that there were severe food shortages almost immediately, so the government brought in food rationing. You registered at your local shops and were given food coupons – how many depended on the number in your household and whether there were children, pregnant women and so on. The shopkeeper was supplied with the exact amount necessary to pass on to his registered customers so, when you went to buy your food, you handed over your coupons as well. Rationed foods were bacon, butter, sugar, meat, tea, jam, biscuits, breakfast cereals, cheese, eggs, milk and canned fruit. At the same time, the government also encouraged a return to farming and home production.

Well, it might surprise you to learn that Britain's men, women and children were at their healthiest recorded weights during this time. With a shortage of fats, sugar and meat, we had to survive on plain rations that relied on unrefined carbs, and vegetables, and we had to make do and eke out. And here's a curious thing – two of the foods that weren't rationed in the war were fish and chips and cocoa (the unsweetened kind, of course, and I suppose you had to like it with water not milk), so it wasn't all bad …

According to the British Nutrition Foundation:

❑ Many people were better fed during wartime food rationing than before the war years. Infant mortality rates declined, and the average age at which people died from natural causes increased.

❑ The wartime food shortages forced people to adopt new eating patterns. Most people ate less meat, fat, eggs and sugar than they had eaten before, but people who had a poor diet before were able to increase their intake of protein and vitamins because they received the same ration as everybody else.

❑ The 'National Loaf' was introduced. It was made with more of the grain than was used in white bread, resulting in a brown loaf. White bread was no longer readily available, and brown bread became the norm.

❑ Special arrangements were made for young children and expectant and nursing mothers to receive cod-liver oil, orange juice and milk from welfare clinics.

When oranges were available, children under six years of age were entitled to receive one pound each week. The general health of children improved and, on average, they were taller and heavier than children before the war.

Now, I don't expect that the wartime diet was anywhere near perfect, but it's interesting that with a reduction in meat, fat and sugar, and a greater reliance on filling carbohydrates and vegetables, people's health and weight began to improve. The result on children is especially interesting in light of the current rise in childhood obesity, and I'm sure that there are lessons in that. It may seem bloody obvious most of the time (too much sugar, fat and processed meat is making our children fat) but something, somewhere, is going wrong.

Is it realistic to think that we could return to a simpler, plainer way of eating that is manifestly much better for us?

To be honest, I doubt it. And, even with world shortages, there's no danger of Sainsbury's running short any time soon. Nevertheless, we have to look seriously at the way we're all eating and why we all feel the need to diet.

Going on about Diets

Q. How much revenue does the diet industry generate in the UK every year?
a) £50 million
b) £200 million
c) £500 million

Hmm. Tricky. It must be £200 million, mustn't it? That sounds reasonable. When in doubt, go for the middle one.

Well, you're wrong. The answer is £2 billion and rising. That is an astronomical figure to spend on something that doesn't really work, isn't it? I mean, if it did, why would we need to go back again and again and again? Have we all got the willpower of craven addicts?

Books, DVDs, hypnotherapy tapes, dieting groups either on-line or en masse, tablets, drinks, cookery books – the list is endless. It seems as if very few of us can do this supposedly simple thing on our own. Why? Is it because we like to pretend it isn't our faults that we're fat? Is our will power really so weak? Or is it just that we'd prefer our DIET – whichever it is – to take responsibility for us, tell us what to do, almost literally spoonfeed us?

Whatever it is, we're making the diet industry very rich indeed. We're also making the associated food industry rich as well. The UK breakfast-cereal industry

– which markets itself almost entirely on health and weight grounds – is worth £1.27 billion per year. Think of all the low-fat, slim-line, weight-watching products there are on the market, all designed to make life easy for people trying to slim, promising to take the effort out of losing weight.

Here's a depressing statistic, and it comes from the diet industry itself: 96 per cent of people who diet will have put on all the weight they lost, if not more, two years after quitting the diet. So it goes on: diet, take off the weight, stop the diet, put the weight back on, diet, take off the weight …

I don't think the industry necessarily wants people to fail – every diet wants to be successful and thus bring more people to it – but it certainly doesn't do it any harm to have people spending their money year after year on its products.

It seems to me that the key to the whole thing lies in the word 'diet' and what it means to us. It seems to imply 'special' eating: this isn't my normal way of doing things, it's my 'diet', and I'm doing it to lose weight. Once I've lost my weight by following my special diet, I'll stop doing it and return to my old ways, the normal way of eating and – oh! Blow me down! I'm putting on weight again … now why would that be? Time to go on a diet again.

The truth is, if you've got fat by getting into the habit

of eating more than you need, you'll never be able to eat in that old way again. If you do, you'll put on weight. Your change in lifestyle has to be permanent. For the rest of your life, you're going to have to be vigilant about what you eat, or you'll put that weight back on.

And that's where so many of us fail.

The diets that appeal to me the least are the extreme low-calorie ones that involve meal packs, shakes, soups and bars. Now, I'm sure that there are people who are in a situation where they need these very low-calorie regimes to make a dent in their weight, and for whom they've worked. I know that some weight-loss programmes offer counselling, on-going support and maintenance advice which try to get to the root of why people overeat. But it's not something for me (not yet, at least, and hopefully never. Just looking at a picture of those shakes is enough to keep me on the straight and narrow). And I've known people who have tried these diets, and they can't stick them for long and I'm not surprised. Imagine coming home after a long hard day, feeling tired, depressed and hungry and look-ing forward to ... a foul-tasting milkshake. Come on! That's not *eating*. It's hardly even existing. It may be for some people, but it's not for me.

The diet industry, though, is fully aware of our need to pamper, spoil and indulge ourselves, and now tries to sell itself by pretending not to offer a 'diet' as such at all: hey, no calorie counting – just follow our simple points systems/eating plans/meal rules and don't miss out on any of the food you love!

But does anyone honestly think they can lose weight while still scoffing as much cheesecake or whatever as they did before? It's obvious that this isn't possible, although lots of us want to believe it is. The Atkins diet seemed like manna from heaven to many people, after years of being told that butter, cream and meat were evil and had to be avoided at all costs: they were seduced by images of butter melting over grilled steaks, plates of creamy scrambled eggs, rashers of bacon, roast chicken with crispy skin ... it looked like the best diet ever.

Except, a low-carbohydrate diet seems to miss out half of what life is all about: steaks – but no fries. Scrambled eggs – but no toast. Chicken – but no roast potatoes. Now, I happen to go along with lots of principles of the Atkins diet: I agree that refined carbohydrates and foods that deliver too much sugar into the system are obviously bad for us, and agree entirely that sugar should be almost absent from our diets. I can also see that this kind of diet can help people with certain medical conditions linked to high blood sugar. But I've also known people who've done Atkins and, in my experience, you don't want to get too close. Besides, any diet that cuts out almost an entire food group (against the advice of most nutritionists) and has to be supplemented with pills to make sure you're getting your nutrients must be slightly suspect.

It seems like a no-brainer to me that any diet should contain all the major food groups, supply all the nutrients, vitamins and minerals we need (unless, of course, there are particular reasons why you're low on something and need supplements), satisfy our hunger and allow us to maintain a healthy weight.

But what *is* that diet? I thought I was following it, with my sensible mix of slow-energy-release carbs, low-fat protein, portions of fruit, vegetables and salad, a small amount of oils and fats and dairy, and healthy snacks.

And yet, I'm not losing much weight, if any at the moment, and I'm still confused about exactly why that is, and what I should be doing.

No wonder so many people turn to a ready-made diet that promises to offer all the answers. At the beginning of all this, I felt complete scorn for the diet industry and the people who couldn't sort out their own weight loss. But now I'm beginning to see that it isn't as easy as I initially thought.

To be honest, I'm beginning to feel tempted myself.

Down at the newsagent's, I find my eye caught by the rows and rows of slimming magazines. I hadn't really thought of these before, but of course they make sense for people who don't have regular access to the internet or can't be bothered trawling through endless websites. At first glance, they all seem to be aimed at women. I check out a couple of the men's mags but it seems that, if you are over thirty (possibly thirty-five at a stretch), you shouldn't be vain enough to worry about your weight. In fact, it seems to be the case that if you don't have abs and are having difficulty seeing over your belly-button, then bad luck, mate, no magazines for you.

While I consider this obvious gap in the market, I buy a couple of diet periodicals and wend my way home.

To my surprise, I find the magazines very interest-ing reading. They are extremely informative, with contact numbers for gyms, nutritional advice and the latest dieting research, exercise guidelines and food-product updates, i.e. what's new and on offer from the different diet companies. To my astonishment, there's a really wide and rather tempting array of diet foods on offer. For example, one company has just updated its range to include, of all things, Ben & Jerry's ice cream and the points value associated with it, so that an ice-cream treat can be worked into a daily food plan, which seems great if you're following that particular plan. Hmm, maybe following a diet wouldn't be so bad after all. Things certainly seem to have changed since I did my rigid Weight Watchers plan all those years ago. I laughed in the face of the idea that you could eat ice cream while on a diet, but maybe it's possible after all.

Another magazine tells you how to cook low-fat

fish and chips, another has recipes for pork biryani and lamb rogan josh. It all looks delicious, and every recipe comes with a handy nutritional guide including the calorific value.

These magazines are a revelation. I suddenly feel quite different about getting help from outside. Like a typical bloke, I thought I could do this entirely alone, and I have, up to a point. Any idiot knows that, if you want to lose weight, you have to eat less and take more exercise. But the human mind is so much more complex than that.

I'm beginning to understand that dieting is about more than just imposing self-control and cutting out refined carbs. It's about examining your relationship with food. I've always known that I was going to be making a permanent change: I can never go back to eating and drinking the amount I was shovelling down my throat before, and I've made a commitment to having exercise in my life from now on.

It's also about accepting help where it's offered. I wonder why on earth there aren't more magazines aimed at men. Maybe they still just won't buy them. But it seems a shame. I've learned a lot from them and have lots more food for thought.

I thought I could do this alone – but maybe I'm going to need more help.

11

A DRY SEPTEMBER

I'm back on track, but it's time to take things up a notch.

I still need to lose two stone and nine pounds. I decide that I'm going to stop drinking completely over September. My experience in France showed me what can happen when I go back to my bad old ways and, although I drank moderately in Turkey, I finally have to admit to myself that it must be the alcohol that's holding me back. I know that alcohol is high in calories but delivers absolutely no nutrients, so it's got nothing to offer my body but weight gain.

And I also have to admit to myself that, although I tell myself I'm drinking one glass of wine, I know that my wine glasses hold quite a lot in them and, sometimes, I have two.

All this is sabotaging my weight loss (still) – and for what?

I enjoy the feeling that alcohol gives me, that glow that gets rid of the stress of a very busy day, and I know I am not alone in that feeling. Most people that I speak to about this have the same sentiment. But I firmly believe that, for most of us, it's just a question of getting into bad habits, rather than becoming seriously addicted. If regular drinking was as frowned upon as smoking is these days, do you think it would be easier to cut down? I do.

I have to ask myself if I have actually been abusing alcohol at some points in my life. The British Heart Foundation recommends that men should drink no more than 3–4 units of alcohol a day. There are 1.5 units of alcohol in a small glass of wine (12.5% ABV, 125ml), half a pint of normal-strength lager, cider or beer, or a pub measure of spirits. I consider that I drink inside those limits most of the time, except that, when I think about it, I realize that when I have a glass of wine it is probably closer to 175ml, and I might have a couple of those, so that's already 4 units, just on a normal night at home. If I decide to party, I'll drink considerably more.

See the table below for the units in typical drinks:

Beer, Lager and Cider	Bottle (330ml)	Can (440ml)	Pint (568ml)	Litre
4%	1.3 units	1.8 units	2.3 units	4 units
5%	1.7 units	2.2 units	2.8 units	5 units
6%	2 units	2.6 units	3.4 units	6 units
'Super-Strength' Drinks	Bottle (330ml)	Can (440ml)	Pint (568ml)	Litre
Beer, Lager and Cider at 9%	3 units	4 units	5.1 units	9 units

Spirits 38–40%	Small measure (25ml)	Large measure (35ml)	Small double measure (50ml)	Large double measure (70ml)
Gin, rum, vodka and whisky	1 unit	1.4 units	1.92 units	2.72.8 units

Wine (red, white, rosé and sparkling) and Champagne	Small glass (125ml)	Standard glass (175ml)	Large glass (250ml)	Bottle (750ml)
10%	1.25 units	1.75 units	2.5 units	7.5 units
11%	1.4 units	1.9 units	2.8 units	8.3 units
12%	1.5 units	2.1 units	3 units	9 units
13%	1.6 units	2.3 units	3.3 units	9.8 units
14%	1.75 units	2.5 units	3.5 units	10.5 units

And the scary thing is that I don't feel as though I'm drinking too much. But I plainly am.

What Harm Does Drinking Do?

The health risks associated with alcohol are serious, as I expect you already know. It takes the liver one hour to process one unit of alcohol, so if you hit it with two or three units in sixty minutes, you're already putting it under strain.

Naturally, once you're drunk, you're at risk of many accidents, simply because you're less inhibited and sometimes have an inflated sense of your own abilities. Once

I've had a few drinks, I know it's kicking in when I begin to feel like the world's best groover. If someone were to show me a video of what I actually look like, no doubt I'd be mortified. But, in the world of booze, I'm better than John Travolta in his glory days. Once you're intoxicated, you're far more likely to trip over, fall down stairs, get into fights or place yourself in dangerous situations.

Even if you're just at home, the risk of accidents is greatly heightened. And that's before you suffer from impotence (the infamous brewer's droop), slowed breathing and heartbeat, and passing out cold.

A hangover is a sign of a body in crisis – the torpor, nausea and headaches are all evidence of how your body is coping with the battering you've given it. Severe dehydration is a consequence of too much alcohol, as is low blood sugar, which is why you might crave water, sweet tea or sugary drinks. Low concentration, irritability, mood swings and even depression will also follow, making it hard to do a job satisfactorily. At its worst, a hangover will incapacitate you, and you will have to sleep it off. More bad news: older drinkers are more likely to suffer ill effects, due to an age-related decrease in body-water content and an increase in body-fat content. That means you get higher blood-alcohol concentration for the same amount of alcohol consumed.

Regular over-drinking takes its toll on the body over time. Few of us suffer the consequences at once, which is why it's so easy to keep at it. For years, you can feel as though it's easy to bounce back, or that your tolerance is high. But, underneath, it's all going on. According to NHS statistics, 6,000 deaths from coronary heart disease in men each year are directly due to alcohol. And I quote: '400 of the 1,700 deaths from mouth cancer per year are linked to heavy drinking – that's nearly one in four.'

The NHS reports that, in England and Wales, alcohol leads to some 33,000 hospital admissions each year for alcohol-related liver disease, i.e. cirrhosis. That's before we get to the other goodies:

- ❏ Cancer, especially mouth and breast cancer (incidents are rising in men, as well as women)
- ❏ Strokes and cardiovascular problems
- ❏ Memory loss, brain damage and even dementia
- ❏ Stomach damage – pancreatitis and gastritis
- ❏ High blood pressure
- ❏ Impotence and fertility problems
- ❏ Mental-health problems
- ❏ Severe alcohol poisoning and death

And, once again, the older you get, the more the risks increase. According to the NHS, you may notice such lovelies as smaller genitals, a lower sperm count, loss of body hair, skin problems and weight gain. Mmm, delightful. For women, there can be irregular periods and lower fertility, and alcohol in pregnancy can wreak terrible damage on an unborn child.

There's no question but that alcohol has a widespread and destructive impact on our society, but drinking seems to be deeply embedded in our culture. So much of our social life revolves around drinking. It's always been this way, and heavy drinking of alcohol has always been particularly rife in socially deprived areas. Nevertheless, the way that young people from all backgrounds – and particularly women – are taking to drinking, especially in the form of binge-drinking (i.e. drinking to get drunk) on Friday and Saturday nights, is very worrying indeed. Young men drink twice what their grandfathers drank, according to the NHS. And 35 per cent of men aged sixteen to twenty-four say they drink more than 8 units on at least one day a week, compared to 18 per cent of those aged forty-five to sixty-four. Since 1979, alcohol-related deaths have almost tripled among men and almost doubled among women.

All this helps me to think again about my own drinking. I'm horrified that our nation is becoming so soaked in booze – no wonder our reputation abroad is so poor – but I know that I'm guilty of treating alcohol thoughtlessly. I don't simply drink with a meal, though I enjoy that, but I use a glass of wine as a reward at the end of a long day or as a way to escape stress. I've got into the habit of thinking that it's perfectly all right to drink every day.

I have to change my mindset about this, just as I have about food and eating. It's all about the attitude, I realize that now – and that realization makes me stronger. On the NHS website, I find a rather interesting list of myths about alcohol. See below to find out what they are.

MYTHS ABOUT ALCOHOL
(Source: www.units.nhs.uk)

MYTH: Alcohol gives you energy, it's a stimulant
TRUTH: Alcohol is a depressant that affects the central nervous system, and can actually make you sleepy. Although the initial effects may seem stimulating, cumulatively, it slows down the way you think, speak, move and react.

MYTH: Beer before liquor, never been sicker/liquor before beer, you're in the clear, or: Beer before wine you'll feel fine/ Wine before beer, you'll feel queer
TRUTH: These urban legends just aren't true. Your blood-alcohol content is what determines how drunk you are. It doesn't matter what type of alcohol you choose – a drink is a drink, and too much of any combination can make you sick.

MYTH: I can sober up quickly if I need to, with a cold shower/fresh air/hot coffee

TRUTH: Taking a shower, drinking ten cups of coffee or eating a loaf of bread will not make you sober. Only time will remove alcohol from your system; depending on your weight, it takes about one hour to eliminate one unit of alcohol.

MYTH: Drink-drivers can be safe, because they drive extra carefully so they don't get pulled over

TRUTH: In 2002, alcohol was involved in 41 per cent of all fatal crashes (NIDA). You might think you're in control, but alcohol slows down reaction time, which makes driving a car much trickier than you think – even if you've only had one drink.

MYTH: Alcohol makes sex better

TRUTH: Alcohol can make people feel less uncomfortable in a social situation. But it can prevent men from getting or keeping an erection, and it can lower women's sex drive too. More importantly, alcohol can affect your decision-making ability: you might put yourself in a risky situation and think you're ready to have sex when you're not or you might not use a condom, putting you at greater risk of a sexually transmitted disease or an unwanted pregnancy.

MYTH: The worst thing that can happen if I drink too much is getting my stomach pumped

TRUTH: Alcohol poisoning can cause death. Also, if you're drunk and unconscious, you could inhale fluids from your vomit, resulting in death by asphyxiation. Long-term, heavy use of alcohol can lead to addiction (alcoholism), and can even cause a heart attack or stroke.

MYTH: Beer gets you less drunk than other drinks
TRUTH: A pint of typical-strength beer (ABV 5 per cent), a glass of wine (250ml, ABV 11 per cent) or a large double vodka (70ml) and coke (ABV 38–40 per cent) are all equally intoxicating, at around 2.8 units of alcohol. It's the alcohol itself, not the type of drink it's found in, that makes you drunk, although, the faster you drink and absorb the alcohol, the higher your peak blood level.

MYTH: Switching between beer, wine and spirits will make you more drunk
TRUTH: Mixing types of drinks may make you sicker by upsetting your stomach, but not more intoxicated.

MYTH: Eating a big meal, or 'coating' your stomach, before you drink will keep you sober
TRUTH: Drinking on a full stomach, or coating your stomach with a greasy or milky solution (like drinking milk before you go out) will only delay the absorption of alcohol into the bloodstream, not prevent it. However, it is best to eat a proper meal before a night out, especially foods rich in carbohydrates and proteins.

MYTH: Your body develops a tolerance to alcohol if you drink a lot regularly, so you can safely drink more
TRUTH: The more you drink, the more damage your body will sustain, and the greater the risks become. Tolerance is actually a warning sign that your body has started to be affected by alcohol.

Tips on Cutting Down

It may be that, like me, you've got into the bad habit of drinking every night at home after work. If so, a few handy tips can help to reduce your weekly intake.

- ❑ Try and have at least one or two days a week completely free of alcohol.
- ❑ If you crave a drink at the same time every night, try having a big glass of water or squash or making a cup of tea – that's often enough to make the craving go away.
- ❑ If you're out and drinking, try and alternate alcoholic drinks with soft drinks.
- ❑ Try and do something else active while you're drinking – such as darts, pool, dancing, if you're out. It will cut down how much you take in.
- ❑ Have a single measure of spirits or small glass of wine topped up with lots of mixer, such as tonic or soda, so that your drink will last longer.

- ❑ Use smaller wine glasses!
- ❑ Drink water during the evening and before you go to bed.

Incidentally, if what I'm saying about drinking is striking a chord with you directly, and you feel that you want to cut down but you may need more help than these tips, go to your local alcohol help centre (listed in your telephone directory), call 0800 876 6776 (textphone 0800 027 4114) or visit your GP. If you are a heavy drinker and might suffer alcohol withdrawal symptoms, NEVER stop drinking suddenly. Instead, cut down a little and get immediate medical advice.

I decide that I'm going to go cold turkey. That's because I really want to give my weight loss a chance, and it just seems easier to cut the stuff out altogether.

Tanya reminds me of the power of visualization and positive thinking. When I want a drink, I should imagine my poor liver trying to process it, the weight gain and the risk of cancer. If that's not enough to put me off, I don't know what is.

Sobriety, here I come …

12

NOW, ABOUT THAT BODY MASS INDEX ...

I've been away from 'the Bastard' – sorry, Imran, my highly respected trainer – for quite a few weeks now, but it's time to get back in the saddle.

During my training, I'm focusing almost entirely on getting my heart rate up and keeping it up for a minimum of twenty minutes. First I run for twenty minutes, then cycle for another twenty, then box for the final twenty, before a stretch out and a warm-down. I'm doing this at least twice a week, three when I can fit it in, and I'm getting in a swim now and then as well.

I'm beginning to appreciate how much exercise is improving my life. I'm seeing a significant change in my body – my stomach is definitely smaller, and my stamina levels have increased fivefold. When I finish a workout, I'm tired, very sweaty and exhausted, but I'm recovering more quickly. I know I look better. My friends tell me I look better, my clothes are fitting better and, do you know what, I feel better too. I might not have shed pounds, but I look different. Standing in front of the mirror, as I did nine months ago, I'm no longer faced with a grey-skinned, red-eyed, old-looking guy carrying extra flesh just about everywhere. I'm healthier, bright-eyed and definitely trimmer. I'm losing inches even though I'm not losing pounds.

Imran reminds me that muscle is heavier than fat, so it's possible to lose fat but maintain your weight, or even increase it.

That might explain some of my slow weight loss.

But, hold on a second, what about my Body Mass Index? That's calculated on how much I weigh, isn't it? If my body is carrying heavy muscle instead of lots of fat, doesn't that make me healthier? And yet, my BMI hasn't changed.

I do a bit of research (thank you, good old internet) and am astonished with what I discover. The Body Mass Index has been used to analyse weight for over a hundred years, since it was devised by Belgian statistician Adolphe Quetelet. But plenty of modern experts are pointing out the drawbacks of the BMI, the main one being that it doesn't take account of whether the body mass is made up of fat or muscle. So a rugby player can be defined as obese while someone who's lighter but actually has more body fat can come in on the healthy range.

Nutritionists and academics now argue that it is how and where fat is distributed on the body that counts. To put it bluntly, if you have a lot of fat around your middle, you're potentially at risk from obesity-related diseases. The newest thinking is that it is the inches around your waist that matter more than your BMI. A waist measurement of more than 88 centimetres (35 inches) in women and 102 centimetres (40 inches) in men indicates the highest risk of cardiovascular disease.

According to one article I read, some critics even believe that when people exercise regularly and have a generally healthy diet and lifestyle, weight itself isn't all that important. It's certainly better to maintain a stable weight than to inflict yo-yo dieting on your system.

Dr Paul Campos, author of *The Obesity Myth*, goes further and is convinced that how much you weigh is almost irrelevant. He thinks we've all become obsessed with weight and the stringent, inaccurate boundaries of the Body Mass Index whereas, in fact, we ought to be focusing on fitness. After all, who is really healthier – a skinny couch potato or a heavier person who does a good hour's cardiovascular exercise every day?

In an article in *Good Health* magazine, Dr Campos is quoted as saying: 'Concentrating on people's weight is a big mistake. The culprit of health problems associated with weight is a sedentary lifestyle and poor nutritional practices, not the weight itself, except in extremely obese cases.'

All this makes sense to me. It seems obvious that it's

possible to be healthy while being heavier than the BMI indicates. After all, my BMI is 32, which is in the obese category, and yet, in my Cardio Direct report, it's clear that I'm fit, with low cholesterol and a small likelihood of any imminent heart problems.

This is all good stuff, and cheering. But I know that I still want to reduce my weight. Common sense is telling me, though, that if I continue to keep exercise in my life and maintain a healthy eating approach, then I'm going to lose weight (probably) and keep this great glow and sense of well being that I'm enjoying.

I'm still cutting out alcohol, though. The Demon Drink has been banished at last.

Two weeks into my dry September, and I've lost two pounds. I'm at fifteen stone. Just like that. I'm really pleased and feel a new rush of enthusiasm. I decide to look again at my diet, as cutting out alcohol is having some unforeseen side effects. For example, my sweet tooth is definitely less apparent. I'm craving sweet things a lot less. In fact, I'm craving less food in general, even though my energy levels have increased, and I'm sleeping well.

I've also cut down on my snacking. I was bringing huge tubs of nuts and dried fruit into work and eating masses when I needed an energy boost. Then it occurred to me that both of these foods are very high in energy – i.e. calories – and it might be that they were contributing to my initial slow weight loss. Now I'm snacking on fruit like apple wedges or raisins, and vegetable snacks like carrot batons. That takes a bit of organization and I can't say I look forward to them with quite as much relish as I did my delicious dried fruit, but the rewards are beginning to show.

The strangest thing about not drinking alcohol is that I don't feel as though I'm missing it at all. I also feel as though I'm on a mission, and that I'd let myself down if I had a drink. It would be a big step backwards. Instead, I drink tea in the morning, about three or four cups of coffee during the day (though I need to be aware of over-doing the cafferine, which can have harmful side-effects if you drink too much of it) and, in between, I'm drinking lots of water, straight and fizzy. Getting myself a big glass of sparkling water, sometimes jazzed up with a bit of lime cordial, sets on me on a great path for an alcohol-free evening. But I'm so determined now. It's taken me a long while to get this far and, if I went backwards again, like I did in July, I would have to make a huge attempt at recovery. By cutting it out of my life completely, I find that the temptation is gone. I don't even think about it. That's me, I suppose. All or nothing ...

I'm living a plain life, it must be said. Yesterday was a typical day.

Breakfast:	Large bowl of reduced fat Quaker granola cereal with semi-skimmed milk and a cup of tea, also with semi-skimmed milk
Mid morning:	Coffee with skimmed milk
Lunch:	Chicken and salad wrap, a bottle of fizzy water
Snack:	An apple
	Coffee with skimmed milk
Supper:	Steamed chicken in a pitta bread, and a salad of lettuce, tomatoes, cucumber, radish and a dressing of oil and vinegar
	Fruit salad of strawberries, kiwi fruit, grapes, apple, blueberries and clementines, with a scoop of live yoghurt

The strange thing is that I don't feel deprived, or as though I'm missing out on something. Instead, I'm enjoying natural flavours and the wonderful sweetness that fruit can offer me. I can see all the things on offer when I go into a sandwich shop – the sandwiches bursting with fatty fillings, the cakes, brownies, croissants, biscuits and chocolate bars. I'm not such a saint that I don't appreciate that a lot of those things taste very nice indeed, and I fully intend to eat those things again at some point in my life – in moderation. But there is no longer any place for eating a bar of chocolate or a sugary, fatty cake that will deliver a shot of sugar into my system and then leave me feeling flat and wanting more, EVERY DAY. I eat when I'm hungry, but I won't eat crap, and that's that. And when I do eat, I don't feel that I'm missing out, because I make sure that I eat a lunch of a good size that will deliver me the energy I need.

At my next weigh-in, I'm 14 stone 13lb. YEE-HAH! I'm under the magic fifteen-stone mark.

I think I really have succeeded in changing my mindset. I feel as though this lifestyle change is permanent, even the lack of alcohol – who knows? But I also know that I'm going to have to guard against getting complacent and thinking that I've won the battle. That's when bad habits start creeping back in, slowly, slowly, without you really noticing it. That's when a 'just this once' treat turns into a daily occurrence.

I don't want to give the impression that I'm suddenly perfect. I'm trying really hard at the moment, because I have a goal in sight and I'm determined to reach it (partly because, if I don't, I'm going to look one hell of an idiot, considering how public my weight loss is). When I feel as though I need a boost, I put my iPod on and relax to a bit of Paul McKenna, or I use one of my hypnotherapy techniques – that stuff really helps me: I don't know why, but it does. Perhaps it just helps me refocus and reaffirm in my own mind what I want to do.

But I can't see into the future. I don't know how I'm going to feel next month, or the month after that. This feeling of control might slip away: I might face some kind of crisis or difficult situation, and who knows what will happen to my resolve then? I hope that I'd be able to stay strong, but I can't be certain I will.

The point is that we all slip up occasionally. A few people with absolutely iron resolve might be able to control themselves day after day for a lifetime, but the rest of us mortals usually can't. With a little encouragement, though, we get up and start again. We might be tempted to think 'Loooser!' and give up, but we mustn't – we shouldn't abandon all the hard work, we should get back on track and praise ourselves for our fortitude and resolve, and keep going.

Here endeth the lesson.

13

THE 'C' WORD

I've set myself the goal of losing three stone by January 2009.

I started out in May 2008, and it's now October 2008. In five months, I've lost just over a stone. While that might not sound like much, it averages out at just over a pound a week, and that's pretty near a perfect weight loss, as recommended by the experts. I haven't denied myself, or gone hungry, or cut out a major food group, but I've reduced sugar, refined carbs and alcohol, and introduced regular exercise into my life – I'm exercising a minimum of two and a maximum of four times a week, with between forty and seventy minutes of cardio a time. I'm following my self-created diet, and I've stayed with my decision to give up alcohol for the duration. Once or twice a week, I weigh myself, and I'm losing weight at that slow but decent rate of around a pound a week, sometimes a bit over, and sometimes a bit under. It's averaging out at a steady weight loss, just as I wanted, based on a sustainable diet.

But I want to speed up my weight loss, just a bit. After all, it's the end of September, and I'm 14 stone 13lb. That's great, of course it's great. I'm pleased. But, if I carry on this way, I will lose the rest of my 34 pounds by mid-June 2009, a year and one month after I started.

That's good and sensible and proves the rightness of everything I've been doing so far. But I really, really want to up my weight loss. I want to see some faster changes. Ideally, I want to be 12 stone 12lb by the second week of January. That means losing 27lb in sixteen weeks, or over a pound and a half a week. That's a significant increase on what I'm losing at the moment. How am I going to do that?

Face to Face with the Dreaded 'C' Word

I've been resolute so far about my decision to avoid the 'C' word. You know the one I mean. Yep. *Calories.* From what I understand, a calorie-controlled diet means weighing out every scrap of food, or using portion pots or whatever, and counting up the calories in every morsel that passes your lips.

It sounds miserable, to be honest, as does recording everything I eat. I mean, who has the time to do that?

But, I also know that no diet in the world is going to work if you consume more energy than your body is taking in. If you do that, you're going to get fat. All diets are either calorie controlled, or designed in such a way that you'll eat filling foods and feel less hungry and, therefore, so the theory goes, eat less.

From what I understand, the recommended daily intake for a man is 2,500 calories. I've picked up that information from the back of food packets and such like. Beyond some vague notions, I have no real idea of the calorific value of foods – I know that sugar and fat and alcohol are high in calories, but that's about it. I certainly have no idea whether I take in 2,500 calories or not.

Actually, when I think about it, I realize that my entire approach to eating is taken from a ragbag of knowledge I've accumulated over the years and based on vague ideas of what's healthy and what's not.

I realize that it's madness to accept the basic premise that it's the number of calories you eat per day that determines your weight and then completely ignore that factor when trying to lose weight. I remember a television programme I saw earlier in the year which analysed the diets of people who were too fat and too thin. The astonishing thing was the diets of the thin people: they were eating absolute rubbish – pies, pasties, biscuits, doughnuts, chocolate, crisps – and yet they were still skinny. But the reason was that, although they were eating high-calorie, fat-laden junk all the time, they ate nothing else. They were still eating under the amount of calories their bodies required every day, so they were thin. Some of the fat people ate the same junk, but their portions were double or triple what the thin people ate, so they were eating well in excess of what their bodies needed. Result: fat, and lots of it. And it wasn't just the people who ate rubbish who were overweight. One woman ate a mouth-watering diet of fresh, home-cooked foods which supplied her handsomely with all the food groups and excellent nutrition, but she was enormous because the size of her portions was vast. The lesson is: you can eat the healthiest, nutritionally perfect diet in the world but if you eat more than you need, you'll put on weight.

To get a bit of basic information about calories, I decide to find out a little more about exactly how my theories of weight loss and good eating stack up against the science. First of all, how many calories a day do I need?

When I do an internet search, hundreds of results come up. Not surprisingly, I'm not the only person who's interested in finding out a bit of information on calories and weight loss. If I needed evidence of our society's obsession with weight, here it is. I click on a free calorie calculator to try and determine my daily intake needs. The calculator needs my weight in kilos

(14 stone 13lb is 209lb, which, at a conversion rate of 1lb = 2.2kg, makes 94.8kg), my sex and my activity levels.

Oh. The calorie calculator says I need 3,185 calories per day. That seems a lot more than the government guidelines. Why is that?

A bit more research on the internet turns up some more facts. The calorie intake I need is defined by my current weight. Put simply, I'm overweight and therefore need more calories so that I have enough energy to keep my body going. If I were at my ideal weight, fewer calories would be needed to maintain my smaller body. But, if I were doing a lot of exercise and had lots of lean muscle (rather than fat), I would need more calories again, as muscle burns calories even while it's resting while fat … um … doesn't.

Okay, got that. It seems a bit counter-intuitive at first, but it makes sense.

It takes a deficit of 500 calories per day over a week to burn off one pound of fat. That doesn't sound too bad at all. If I need 3,185 calories to maintain my weight, then I need around 2,600 to lose a pound a week. If I wanted to lose two pounds per week, I'd need to create a deficiency of 1,000 calories per day. I'm still in the dark about exactly how many calories are in what, but a diet of 2,185 calories per day sounds suspiciously little to me. It sounds a bit close to feeling hungry all the time and having to suffer while counting calories.

That is most definitely not for me. I stick by my theory that it is perfectly possible to lose weight and not endure horrible hunger pangs and feelings of deprivation. It must be.

During my internet searches, I keep stumbling across a website that is essentially a tool for counting calories. It offers quite a lot of free information, explaining how that calorie deficit works, and promises that its food-diary tool makes keeping track of calories easy. It also offers nutritional information, charts your goals and weight loss and has recipes and tips and a forum for members to chat on.

It looks quite interesting, and I decide that I'll do a twenty-four-hour free trial, put my day's menu through the counter and see how it stacks up. After all, it can't do any harm, and knowledge is power. I'm curious now to find out how my self-made diet fares.

I sign up for my free trial and the site asks me to fill in my basic details.

Height: 5 feet 7 inches
Weight: 14 stone 13lb
Activity: moderately active. The site tells me not to count specific exercise at this point, as I'll put that into my exercise diary.

The calculator tells me that my ideal weight range is 9 stone 12lb to 11 stone 5lb, based on – you guessed it – the Body Mass Index. At 14 stone 13lb, my BMI is 32.7. You know how I feel about BMI – I'm distinctly unconvinced. I may not be the tallest bloke in the world; but in my time I've been very muscly and fit, and I can tell you that if I ever got down to 9 stone 12lb, I would look ill. My frame isn't like that. Being that thin just wouldn't suit me.

But the calculator also says it's up to me to find the weight I feel happiest at, which is reassuring.

At the next stop, I'm asked if I want to lose weight, or maintain weight. I choose lose weight, of course, and then it asks for my target weight. I put in 12 stone 12lb. Now I'm prompted to say how fast I want to lose it. The options are: 0.5lb, 1lb, 1.5lb, 2lb.

I put in 1.5lb. That seems sensible and probably not too difficult to cope with.

Instantly, my daily calorie allowance appears. It is … 2,177 calories per day. Well, maybe that isn't so bad. I've got it into my head that the daily rate for men is 2,500 so that's only 323 calories less than that. So it can't be so hard, can it? I wonder if I've been eating a lot more calories than I've realized. That thought is faintly depressing.

To see my experiment through, I enter everything I've eaten today into the food diary. Here goes … The site has a food database, which is a bit fiddly to use at first, until I begin to learn how to find my way around. There are lots and lots of branded products, which must make your life easier if you do all your food shopping at the supermarket and eat a lot of ready-made products. If you don't, you need to find the basic version of your food and then work out what kind of a portion you've had. This means – yuk – weighing it. Something I vowed I'd never do. But, in the interest of the pursuit of knowledge, I decide that I will do this and, actually, I'm quite interested now to find out what my calorie intake is. I have to do some estimating, of course, as I can't weigh food I've already eaten, but I decide to err on the side of caution and overestimate rather than underestimate, so that I don't give myself a falsely optimistic picture.

All the foods you add are automatically filed in your personal database, so you don't have to start from scratch every time. And another good way to work out calories is the recipe feature: if you're cooking a casserole, you enter all the ingredients and how many servings you get from it, and the site works out what the calorie content is per portion. Basically, the more you use the calculator, the more use it will be.

I'm quite impressed – it seems like a useful tool for someone who is calorie counting and a much more cool and sophisticated way to go about it than I'd imagined. I also like the way your allowance per day is yours to do with what you will. If you want to eat cake or whatever, fine, just put it in. The effect on your calorie quota might make you think twice before you do that too often, but no one is going to criticize or judge or tell you you've sinned.

Here are the results from my food diary ...

BREAKFAST:

Big bowl of oat granola (100g)	410 calories
Mug of tea with semi-skimmed milk	19 calories
Semi-skimmed milk on cereal (100ml)	50 calories

So breakfast comes in at 479 calories. Not bad. And, apparently, I have 1,698 calories left for the rest of the day, which seems okay to me.

SNACK:

Medium-sized banana	116 calories
Two cups of coffee with skimmed milk	32 calories

That brings my tally up to 627, with 1,550 left for the rest of the day. That seems plenty to me.

LUNCH:

A tin of John West Salmon Light Lunch, Moroccan style	200 calories
Water	

I did have a very light lunch today, so I'm saving calories on that. I'm pretty sure my usual lunch would be more likely to be up round the 300 mark, probably more.

SNACK:

Handful of dried figs	347 calories
Apple	80 calories
Cup of coffee with skimmed milk	16 calories

I'm surprised by the amount of calories in the dried figs. Apart from breakfast, they're the most calorific thing I've eaten today. I remember how much concentrated natural sugar there is in dried fruit – I'll have to watch out for that. Still, I'm only up to 1,270 calories, well under my ration for the day.

DINNER:

A medium fillet of salmon pan-fried in olive oil	274 calories
Salad of lettuce, tomatoes, cucumber, radish	82 calories
Dressing of oil and vinegar	71 calories
Big bowl of fruit salad: strawberries, blueberries, grapes, kiwi, apple and clementines	321 calories
Big spoonful of organic, low-fat natural yoghurt	77 calories
Glass of lime cordial and water	22 calories

My dinner totals 847 calories, which also surprises me, considering how healthy it looks on paper. The main course comes in at 427, and the rest is my pudding. Still, it's my main meal of the day, and provides me with a major helping of nutrients.

Well – what do you know? I'm under my calorie allowance.

To maintain my current weight, I need to eat 2,929 calories. If I eat less than that each day, I'll lose weight. If I eat at a rate of 2,177 calories day, I'll lose 1.5lb a week, which is my goal. And guess what … today's food comes in at 2,120, 57 calories *under* my quota. RESULT!!

But I did have a very light lunch … what if I'd had a slightly heavier lunch, as I often do? Or the second small breakfast I sometimes eat after training? That would put me well over the desired quota. As for what would happen if I were still drinking, I dread to think. Just out of interest, I put in a large glass of white wine. A 175ml glass puts on 115 calories. A 250ml glass stacks on 165 calories. But a bottle puts on 495 calories – the equivalent of another whole meal – or two and a half times my lunch.

No wonder I was getting fat.

Thinking about my exercise, I go to the exercise section and enter my thirty minutes running on the treadmill, which I do on a couple of the mornings that

I'm not training with Imran. I try and go at quite a whack. The site comes up with a figure of 500 calories that I burn off during that session, and promptly adds those calories to my daily quota.

Brilliant. On the days I don't exercise, I can eat lightly and stay inside the limit I need to keep losing weight. On the days I do exercise, I can eat more heartily – and I need to, because I'm hungrier – and still keep losing the weight. Love it.

The thing that is appealing about calorie counting is that it is very straightforward. There are no forbidden foods or combinations. You could eat just crisps all day if you wanted. It's very simple: if you eat fewer calories than your body expends every day, you'll lose weight. But, as soon as you see how those calories add up, you want to make sensible choices, so that you can eat delicious and filling food but keep within your quota.

I remember those recipes I found in the slimming magazines – clever ideas for tasty dinners that don't pile on wasted calories. Perhaps I'll try my hand at a couple of those on a night when I don't feel like plain fish and salad again ...

Then I notice that, on the site, as well as the food diary/calorie counter, there is also a nutrition profile. I take a quick look at how my day has stacked up.

It's laid out like a couple of pie charts, with the percentages in them. One shows the target nutrition profile recommended by the website. The other is my very own intake.

	Target	Fat Bloke
Carbohydrates	55%	63.5%
Proteins	15%	14.6%
Fats	30%	21.9%
Alcohol	0%	0%

Hey! Not bad! Pretty much spot on.

I'm chuffed. I never wanted to count calories, but I've always accepted that, unless I create a deficit between what I take in and what I give out, I'm never going to lose weight. I felt I could do that pretty much instinctively, and putting one day's diet to the test like this has proved me right.

But it's also taught me that I'm going to have to stay vigilant if I want to carry on losing weight. I don't intend to start weighing my food now, or ever, and, to be honest, neither do any of the men I know. I haven't got time for all that. But my mind is open to learning how to cook some meals which are a bit lower in calories, and to ways to trim out unnecessary calories which could be quietly but consistently pushing me over what my body needs and into fat-storage territory.

Using the calorie counter has been interesting, but it's confirmed my belief that if I follow my instincts and keep in control of what I'm eating, keep off the booze and on the treadmill, a lower weight and better health will follow as naturally as night follows day.

14

REAL MEN DON'T DIET?

It's mid October. Time for a weigh-in.

Tanya tells me that I'm looking great – fitter and healthier than I have for years. I know she's right, and I'm delighted with what I've achieved so far. And, sure enough, I've got down to 14 stone 11lb. Another two pounds shaved off my weight. I'm getting close to fourteen and a half stone, which is brilliant. To think that, only a few months ago, I was hurtling up towards sixteen stone, and my body was feeling it badly.

I was out of condition and felt awful: lethargic, morose and ill.

Just bringing my weight down this far has transformed me. There's still a way to go, but I feel as though the hardest step has been taken, and that was to acknowledge my problem and decide to do something about it.

Tanya gives me a draft of an article she has written: it's about childhood obesity, and I agree with everything she's said in it – it's something that needs immediate attention and action. However, it isn't so much the article itself as the effect reading it has on me. As I read, I suddenly become aware of being quite hot, even though the weather is definitely chilly. I put my hand to my forehead and realize that I'm sweating profusely.

I can recognize myself in the article. I was one of those fat children, and just the memory of it makes me anxious and panicked. That's how much my weight and the history of my weight and my perception of how others view me because of my weight (sigh, you can see how much I want to be rid of all this crap!) affects me.

It's strange that, with this kind of baggage, I picked a job where I'm going to be endlessly looked at and commented on, especially when I can hardly bear to look at myself in the mirror. Maybe it was a way of facing my fears and making myself stronger, I don't know. But it seems to me that the way I perceive myself and think about my weight is also deeply influenced by the fact I'm a man.

I started writing this book because, when I decided to take that all-important look in the mirror and see myself – I mean, *really* see myself – I stumbled on a lot of ambivalent feelings.

❏ Am I supposed to care about how I look? I'm a man, right?

❏ It's vain and effeminate to care about how I look.
❏ Real men don't diet. Dieting is for women. That whole world is aimed at women, and it's all about being sexually attractive and better looking. I mean, for god's sake, the manufacturers of Special K don't even bother to put the recommended daily calorie allowance for men on the packet.

Do any of these feelings make sense? Why should being a man mean it's not possible to be honest about my weight problem and the need to do something about it?

Women seem to be able to appraise themselves critically and talk openly about it. They can stand in front of mirror and look at themselves in a detached way, and talk about what they're going to do to get rid of their muffin tops. All right, I can't claim to be an expert on the inner workings of the female mind, and no doubt there are plenty of women who can't do this, but, nonetheless, women seem to be able to recognize their problem and discuss it amongst themselves in a way that men can't.

In my forays into the internet, looking up advice and information on weight and diet, I've found masses of forums and chat rooms where women are talking about their weight and encouraging each other in pursuit of losing the excess pounds and getting healthier. I've found weigh-in clubs who convene at the same time every week to swap results, forums devoted to one particular diet, with extra information, warnings about pitfalls and so on, and sites where people swap recipes and health tips. This all seemed great to me … and yet, I can't see many blokes doing this, just as I can't really imagine your average man going to Weight Watchers or joining Slimmer's World or whatever. Maybe a couple do, but most of us don't. And we don't sit around in the pub talking about our weight, looks and body image (not even actors, who are a pretty narcissistic, self-obsessed bunch at the best of times).

Having said that, I think the internet is an excellent source of information and encouragement for men who'd run a mile rather than see their doctor or talk to someone about their health. See p. 227 for some useful internet sites which could be a good starting point if you're nervous about discussing a problem.

You might say that there is much more pressure on women to be slim and attractive, and I suppose you'd be right. But men are also oppressed by the images of perfection everywhere. Every time I pick up a paper, I see Brad Pitt or some other superstar in his buffed perfection, and the truth is that those images make me feel inadequate. I feel as though I ought to look like that, even though it's impossible, not just because, sadly, I'm never going to be Brad Pitt, but also because I'm not a multimillionaire with a personal chef whose only role in life is to cook nutritionally balanced, low-fat, low-calorie meals for me. And I'm guessing you're not either. We can't compete, just as your average woman can't compete with the idealized images of women (air-brushed completely out of the real world, I might add), with all their hairdressers, make-up artists, high fashion and professional photographers, bombarding us from hundreds of different sources every single day.

But while women see this constant reminder of what they should be as a spur to try harder (too hard, in some cases, when young women become obsessed with an unrealistic body image, and risk their health to achieve it), we men seem to see it as a reason not to bother at all.

What's the point? I'm never going to look like that, so who cares?

A friend of mine has a theory that women still have a primitive need to compete with each other to get the best man for breeding purposes, so they're genetically programmed to care about how they look and to want to look better than the next female. By the same token, the man is programmed not to look at himself but rather to scrutinize the women to find the most fertile (hence the male obsession with breasts, hips, long legs, youthful faces – all indicators of a fertile woman) and make his choice.

Perhaps that's why so many men find it difficult to look at their reflections and assess the way they really look. It's not something they want to confront, or something they're programmed to confront.

I have no real idea what the reason is, all I know is that I've never found it easy to consider my body and what I'm doing to it objectively, and I don't think I'm unusual in that respect.

But that's got to change. Men's health is a ticking time-bomb at the moment. We don't do as much manual labour and physical work as our grandfathers did a couple of generations ago, and yet we eat and drink a great deal more. We sit around almost the whole day but fill our diets with fats and sugars. If we don't become more aware of what we need to do, the outlook for men isn't great. This isn't about looking good in suits (although, obviously, that wouldn't hurt), it's about looking after ourselves so that we actually make it into old age fit enough to enjoy it.

That's where I hope this book can come in and provide some help. When I started my column in the *Daily Mail*, I was amazed by the number of people – men, mostly – writing to me, saying they were in exactly the same position as me. An awful lot of them were doing something about it in the way that suited them best, very often helped along by wives and girlfriends, and were keen to share their own particular way of shedding pounds. Some were inspired to admit to themselves properly what they'd been thinking for ages:

they're overweight and need to do something about it. It's those blokes I'm reaching out to, to tell them that it isn't effeminate to lose weight or care about your appearance. It's completely and entirely necessary, and you will never regret making that decision.

As October progresses, I continue my resolve to stay off the alcohol.

The calorie-counter experiment has taught me how incredibly easy it is to push yourself over what you need without even noticing. Those forgotten calories add up. All you need to do is eat an extra hundred calories a day on top of what you need, and you'll gain weight. It will go on slowly but, at the end of a year, you could be up to a stone heavier, if not more.

Alcohol is full of empty calories, and it doesn't have a place in my diet at the moment. I really don't want to jeopardize what I'm doing, and I know that I can easily scupper my on-going weight loss by getting back into the habit of drinking too much wine. When I'm at my ideal weight, I'll need between 2,500 and 2,800 calories a day, depending on my activity levels. At that point, I'll have room in my life for a bit of drinking and an indulgence on special occasions, but I realize now that my whole mindset about alcohol has changed.

Now I intend to drink wine not to answer an emotional need – I'm tired, I need to relax, I deserve it after a hard day – but as the best accompaniment to a good meal. The French don't understand the way that we British drink so much when we're not eating. I intend to emulate them, and enjoy good wine with my food, and stop drinking for drinking's sake. I'm going to make that a life goal, not just a weight-loss goal.

But until then, I'm still on the wagon.

I also decide to step up my training. The calorie-counter experiment reinforced in my mind the relationship between the activity we do and the energy we require from our food. The equation is such a simple one, and yet all too easy to forget. We eat for a reason: to give us the fuel to exist and be active. In the modern world, we've lost sight of that. We're surrounded by so much food all the time that the term 'obesogenic' has been coined to describe our society. Literally, it means that we live in an environment that encourages obesity. Labour and activity-saving devices – everything from vacuum cleaners, to escalators, to cars, to remote controls – have reduced the amount of activity in our lives. And we are surrounded by food: restaurants, bars, cafés, fast-food outlets, supermarkets packed with cheap, easy-to-prepare ready-meals, and so on.

For evidence of how obesogenic our society has become, just look at the railway stations. It used to be you would have one grotty pub-type place, a café serving nasty tea and coffee in china cups and stainless-steel pots, and maybe fish and chips if you were lucky, perhaps a burger joint if it was really fancy. And some plastic sandwiches in packets at the newsagent's.

Of course I'm pleased that we can finally get our hands on some decent coffee and fresh, well-made food. That's a plus in anyone's book. And there's lots of healthy stuff on offer too (if you don't mind the prices). But there's so bloody much of it.

I was walking through Victoria Station in London the other day, and I saw the following food and drink outlets: Marks & Spencer Simply Food, Starbucks, Prêt à Manger, Camden Coffee Company, a French croissant and baguette outlet, another filled-baguette outlet, a Krispy Kreme Donut stand, a Piece of Cake stand, a Caffè Nero stand, a Thorntons chocolates stand, McDonald's and a pub-style restaurant. That was only in half the station. God knows how much more there was on the other side.

We are surrounded! The message is that we cannot be expected to go anywhere or do anything without mountains of food and drink at all times. It would be amazing if we were immune to all this. All these triggers are telling us to eat or drink and, unless we're hyper-aware, we're going to give into them significantly often.

Our children are growing up in a world in which

they are surrounded by temptation wherever they go. There are vending machines selling chocolate bars in schools! There's one in the lobby of the local gym, just where the kids come out of their soft-play area. The number of tantrums I've seen in front of that thing – screaming toddlers begging for sweets while their mums try to drag them away. How are children supposed to know any better when this kind of stuff is dangled endlessly in front of them? In their world, adults are constantly putting food in front of their noses. They can't walk to school without passing dozens of fast-food joints. Every shop they go into has mountains of sweets and crisps on offer. The supermarket has many more aisles devoted to biscuits, sweets, snacks, ice creams, cakes, frozen pizzas and ready-meals than it does to fresh food.

What on earth are kids supposed to think?

Children need good food and energy to grow. Their young bodies demand high-calorie foods, and they need a good supply of fats along with everything else. They usually adore sugar and sweet things, probably because, in the natural world, sugar occurs in ripe fruits, which are a brilliant source of vitamins. But if that taste for fats and sugars is allowed to get out of control, especially if physical activity is taken out of the equation, we get the results already being seen across the country: fat children with rotting teeth, out of control from their sugar intake, on the road to obesity, diabetes and low educational results.

Their young lives are blighted before they've even started. If we don't get a grip on this problem, a really awful future awaits our children. The figures already make frightening reading. A quarter of all school children in the UK are obese, according to government figures, and the Department for Children, Schools and Families has predicted that half of all children could be obese by 2050.

I believe that kids are programmed to want what they can't have, or shouldn't have – that's what they do. It's our job to say no. We say no not to spoil their fun, but because we're adults and we are responsible for their health and well being, and we should know better. We can say quite firmly, 'If you eat too many cakes/sweets/bags of chips, it's bad for you.' Of course we have to be careful not to be alarmist or start associating food with illness, but there's plenty of good stuff we can encourage them to eat instead. It's not that bloody difficult, is it?

Writing about childhood obesity is always hard for me because of my own history, but it makes me all the more passionate about it. We need to stop children going through the problems of bullying and low esteem, let alone the health issues associated with being overweight. These days, there is simply no excuse. We know better. We know about nutrition, and we know about the ill effects of a bad diet.

I watched a documentary the other night about a man in the States who weighed half a ton. I know I've let my weight get out of control, but how the hell do you let yourself get to half a ton? And didn't someone think to say, 'Hey, Joe, you're getting a bit on the portly side. Do you think maybe you should cut out eating Big Macs and KFC for a while and think about getting off the sofa once in a while?' Of course, by this stage his arse wasn't just fat, it was the size of a small country. And the couch wasn't a couch, it was a reinforced bed-cum-residence which he never left.

The worst part of the documentary I saw was that, while this guy's family was waiting in the hospital while he had his stomach stapled, they ordered themselves a meal. You guessed it – a big, family feast of hamburgers. And the saddest thing about it was that they were feeding it to their six-month-old baby girl. There didn't seem to be any realization that the cycle of overeating junk food and appalling obesity would continue. And that little kid didn't have any choice in the matter.

It brought home to me the extent of our responsibilities as adults. I feel very strongly that we need to do something about the diets of our children, and I applaud every effort being made in that direction, wherever it comes from. I'd prefer it to be from our government, but if it takes celebrity chefs to point out the scandal of kids eating chips and meat reclaimed from animal carcasses for every meal, so be it.

I've gone off at something of a tangent there but, actually, I really needed to get that off my chest.

15

BREAKING THOSE BAD HABITS

My loss at a rate of a pound a week or just over is continuing. I'm at 14 stone 9lb and feeling bloody pleased with myself. But I don't want to slacken now. This weight-loss thing is quite addictive (and, if you haven't spotted it by now, I've got an addictive personality, so I'd better watch out). I can understand for the first time how women can find dieting so engrossing. It's not that I want to climb on the scales twenty times a day – once a week is enough for me – but I get a thrill out of seeing those numbers decrease each time, and a small sense of dread that they might have gone up.

Now I'm down at the gym four times a week. I've got two weekly sessions with Imran, and the other two mornings I'm running on the treadmill and doing some weights – all very good stuff for my overall bone and muscle strength.

Imran reminds me of the importance of pushing myself and continuing to set myself new challenges. He also says that I've got to keep varying my workouts so that my body doesn't become accustomed to a certain kind of regime and stops working so hard.

Tricky things, these bodies, aren't they? They're a lot more cunning than I realized.

Imran sets me new ways of exercising the same muscle sets, and pushes me on to keep doing more. Where I once did a set of twelve push-ups from the hip, I'm now doing a set of twenty from the toes – and three sets of those instead of two. It turns out that these trainers always have a more difficult version of the exercise you've just mastered up their sleeves. When I'm feeling knackered, Imran reminds me of how far I've come and how much more I can achieve than I could when I started out.

'You were one fat bastard,' he tells me, 'but you're doing really good now.'

Maybe his charm doesn't translate so well to the page, but Imran makes me realize that all of us have the capacity to do more than we think. Our bodies will always respond, but only if we make the effort.

The other thing I do in the second half of this month, again linked to my calorie-counter experiment, is to look afresh at my portion sizes.

Right from the start, when I started this weight-loss campaign, I had a theory that it is all about moderation and being able to say 'enough'. Once I'd cut out some of the junk, I was sure that my basic diet was a healthy one. I just needed to make sure I wasn't eating too much of it.

I still stand by that, but it's been harder than I thought. In theory, it's easy but, in reality, cutting down takes a hell of a lot of discipline. I realize that our dinner plates and pasta bowls are enormous, and that I've always filled them to brimming. It's purely psychological – it looks like a filling meal, whereas a half-full plate or bowl does not. So I go out and buy some smaller dishes – not miniature, by any means, but also not enormous. It's a mark of how much of an unnoticed habit overeating can become because, when I start using the smaller dishes, I don't feel any more hungry at the end of a meal than I did with the big plates, but I'm eating just a bit less, saving myself those vital calories every time.

My theory is that very few of us in the modern world eat only because we're hungry. Yes, we do need our three meals a day (or four small meals, or however it best suits you to meet your needs) and, if we don't get them, we'll soon feel and see the effects.

But our emotional connection with food runs deep. Many of us turn to food for comfort and a sense of well being. I once heard someone describe eating a meal of hot food as being given a lovely big hug. She was depressed and needed lots of hugs – and, as a result, she was hugely overweight. We also often associate food with good times. Most of our social occasions revolve around food, and the main festivals of most cultures are celebrated with special foods. That's not surprising, because the need to eat and the pleasure of eating is woven so deeply into our existence.

In this modern world, where food is everywhere, we've lost the balance between feasting and moderation.

Take Christmas, for example. Christmas is a Christian festival, but it took the place of a more ancient, pagan midwinter feast. In the depths of darkness, when the natural world has shut down and stopped producing any food, our ancestors lit candles, hung the mistletoe, burned the pine logs and ate and drank themselves stupid, bringing out all the food they'd stored and prepared for just this occasion.

Later, when the festival had been Christianized and came to last twelve days, it was followed soon afterwards by Lent, a long stretch of austerity, self-denial and plain eating (which coincided with the bare days of February, March and April). Then came the next great festival, Easter, just in time to celebrate longer days, sunshine, the birth of new livestock, and nature's larder being open for business again. After that was a long summer of plenty, with fruits, vegetables and grains, and meat in abundance, and the surplus was bottled, preserved, dried, salted and stored. Then, as the season turned, came the Harvest Festival, time to feast once more on all that bounty, gather it in and start preparing for the cold, hard winter months when the earth closes down, to be lightened in the middle by that wonderful speck of light in the darkness – Christmas.

So far, so nostalgic.

The point is that, in the modern world, we no longer have long periods of abstinence and austerity to balance the times of feasting and overindulgence. The natural rhythm has been lost. For us, it's Christmas every day. For the lucky ones, in the modern western world, our houses are always well lit and warm. The supermarket is always stocked with anything we might desire, no matter what the season, climate or region we live in. Want some mangoes? Here they are. Fancy meat, fish or vegetables out of season? No problem, we've flown it in from halfway round the world. Ever seen a sign up in the supermarket saying, 'As we sold mountains of sweets, chocolates and biscuits at Christmas, we won't be selling any more for a few weeks'?

I'm not saying that's what supermarkets *should* do – they're businesses, not health monitors. I'm saying it's what *we* should do. We need to use a bit of self-discipline and our natural intelligence and bring a bit of balance back into our lives.

If we eat less, we'll appreciate the days of plenty more. If we keep it simple and moderate in the week, we can afford to splurge a bit at weekends. If we eat modestly for most of the year, we'll appreciate even more the big events in our lives – the weddings, christenings, birthdays and so on – which we celebrate with lashings of food and drink.

When I went to France for my sister-in-law's wedding, I went off the rails because, to make the holiday feel special, I ate and drank *more* than I did usually. And, the trouble was, I was already eating and drinking too much.

When I think ahead to Christmas now, I realize that, as I'm not drinking at all, a small amount of alcohol – a glass of mulled wine, a Scotch after dinner or whatever – is going to seem significant. Because I'm eating smaller portions and cutting down on rich food, a huge roast with all the trimmings, plus a rich pudding and brandy butter and maybe chocolates to follow, along with a few glasses of wine, will seem like what it is: a gluttonous overeat that I'll only be able to manage occasionally.

When the big day comes, I'll indulge like everyone else, but the difference is that, this year, I'll feel like I've earned my feast, and I'll be fully aware that, once it's over, it's back to my moderate way of eating, because that's the way that suits me and my body best.

Breaking Habits

So, I've discovered that overeating is partly emotional and partly habit. A big part of being able to lose weight is breaking those connections, and that's all about mind over matter. A friend of mine told me of the saying, 'It takes three weeks to make a habit and three weeks to break a habit.' I definitely agree that it takes time to break a habit. Whether three weeks is enough is another matter – I think it may be a lot longer. Six months to a year maybe, for the really ingrained habits. But, once you've taken the first step, you are on the right path. And the longer you keep on the right path, the easier it will be to stay there.

Now I look back at my old self and I can hardly believe what I used to do. How could I not see how damaging my behaviour was?

I just didn't realize that habits are the result of not thinking. They are habits precisely because we don't really think about we are doing, we just do it. So, the best way to get on top of your bad habits is to start observing your own behaviour and analysing it. What do you do? Why do you do it? Are you really hungry when you eat, or is it some other need you're answering?

A woman I know used to eat a big slice of cake at lunchtime on Tuesdays and Thursdays. She really wanted it, even though she wasn't hungry. Then she realized that what really lay beneath the craving was that she was dreading a particular work meeting she had to attend on those afternoons, and she was giving herself a big sugary treat beforehand so she didn't feel so bad. As soon as she realized that was what she was doing, she was able to get on top of her desire for something sugary and replace it with something else.

Here are some handy tips for breaking bad habits.

❑ **Become aware.** You have to admit to yourself that you've got yourself into bad habits: you're eating a bar of chocolate every day without even noticing/ having two big glasses of wine a night/ buying take-aways three times a week – whatever it is.

❑ **Ask yourself why.** Do you eat chocolate because you feel you need a reward? Or do you enjoy the boost it gives you? Are you like me, and see your glass of wine as a way to relax? What emotional need is answered by the food or drink you're taking in? Once you can see your motivation, the idea of being comforted by a bar of chocolate or a bag of chips can often seem a bit ridiculous, and realizing this will help change your mindset. Remind yourself that your bad habit is no reward – it's actually making you fat and miserable and stopping you from enjoying life.

❑ **Decide to change.** It sounds simple, and of course

it's not, but, without making the decision to change, you won't ever manage it. It's up to you. If you know you need a 'reward', decide to change the reward. If, for you, a Ryvita with honey is never going to replace a KitKat, perhaps change the terms of your reward system – for example, tell yourself: I will only have a KitKat on Saturday nights, and I will look forward to and enjoy that KitKat more than any of the six or seven a week I've been eating without even noticing them.

Or go cold turkey and give it all up completely. That's what I've done with my glasses of wine.

Do your will power a favour and get rid of anything in the house that might tempt you, or at least put it out of sight. Don't let it call to you from wherever you've hidden it, or from the corner shop, or wherever it is. Tell it firmly to shut up and go away, because you're not giving in.

❑ **Stick with it.** Once again, it sounds easy but it isn't. You have to use some self-discipline to break habits, and there's no way I can make that sound less tough. Every day you'll have to tell yourself that you're not going to give in to the urge that tells you to have that chocolate bar, or whatever it may be. It will get easier over time, and the first few days will definitely be the hardest. Avoid putting yourself in situations where you'll be tempted – perhaps don't go out with friends for a while, if that's your trigger for overindulging in food or drink, or suggest the cinema instead of the pub.

Sometimes, you'll decide that it's just not worth it and give in – don't beat yourself up or start hating yourself. Those feelings are only going to make it more likely that you'll go back to your bad habits. Pick yourself up and start again, this time with renewed resolve. Hold on to how good you feel when you stay strong. Imagine the day coming when you'll be so used to not eating that chocolate, you won't even think about it …

❏ **Ask for help if you need it.** Blokes are bad at this. If you're struggling, try an internet chat room. You'll be amazed at how many people are attempting to break bad habits, just like you. One of the strengths of diet groups is that they help you realize that you're not alone. You're not weak, greedy, flawed and useless – you're human, and you're doing your best. Encouragement and praise work just as well on adults as on children. Always remember that you'll have to stay strong – it's easy to slip back without even realizing it because you think you've conquered that bad habit. Try and stay aware and alert. Taking a step back and seeing your own behaviour is key.

Perhaps the most important lesson I've learned in this whole weight-loss exercise is that it's a question of mind over matter. Most of your decisions are made by your head, not your stomach. Once you understand that you're in charge and in control and, more importantly, that *you want to change*, you can do it. I have, and I'm a fat bloke with a taste for booze, a distaste for mirrors and a tendency towards addictive behaviour. If I can do it, so can you.

I promise.

16

SUCCESS AT LAST ...

I hope I haven't spoken too soon.

Here's a report from the Fat Bloke Front Line:

Date:	Early November
Weight:	14 stone 4lb. Yessss!!!
Target:	20lb to go
Time to left to target:	11 weeks
Rate of loss necessary:	Just under 2lb per week

That's a big weight loss still to go. I want to do it, and I will, near as dammit, have lost three stone come January.

The strange thing about this book is that it's going to end before my diet does. The realities of book publishing mean that I have to stop writing before I know for sure if my weight loss is going to be a success or not. I think it will be, but it's like jumping off a cliff into the dark.

What if I don't do it?

I guess huge public humiliation is an incentive of a kind that most people don't have, so I have to put my faith in my resolve not to look a total fool.

But I've also put my faith in my new lifestyle. I have to keep reminding myself not to use the word 'diet' because that's not what I've done. I haven't come up with a 'diet' that tells you exactly what you need to eat and lays out menus for you to copy.

My guess is that, if you're anything like me, you might stick to a menu plan for about ... ooh ... a day and a half? Before you think, Sod it, I can't be bothered ... and stop.

So this is what I did:

- ❑ I took the decision to change some of what I eat – no more junk, no more splurging on refined carbs, no more sugar.
- ❑ I decided to think about what I eat and drink, eating *more* of the good stuff (whole, slow-release carbs, lean proteins, fresh fruit and vegetables) and *less* of the bad stuff. (I still have takeaways, but I'll skip the naan and go for plain rice and no creamy sauces.)
- ❑ I cut out my weak spot: alcohol.
- ❑ I tried to make my portions smaller, but not so small I'd feel deprived or hungry.
- ❑ I started exercising.

You can do these simple things too, and they will make a difference. But everyone is different. You may worry that cutting out your favourite foods will simply make you crave them and then you'll binge. If so, decide to eat much less of them, but don't deny yourself completely.

Thinking about your food and monitoring your intake will be something you do to suit you. I kept track of what I was eating for this book, and that was the spur I needed. If you're finding it hard to keep a record of your intake and you need to examine where your weak spots are, you may need to find your own method. I've never been one for in-depth food diaries, but some people find them invaluable. If you think this might help you, give it a go. Buy yourself a nice smart notebook, or join an internet weight-loss site, and start recording everything you eat and drink. It will show you where you're taking in your calories and how often you're eating without even noticing it. Being aware is the first step to changing, after all.

You might be tempted to cheat and not put down that extra glass of wine, or that quick toastie you snaffled down. That's fine – but, remember, the only person you cheat on is yourself. And what's the point of that?

Have a think about your nutrition: are you eating those five portions of fruit and vegetables each day? Aim for two of fruit and three of vegetables. Add some greenery or veg to your lunch if you can, and finish with a piece of fruit. Don't be seduced by the fashionable message that carbs are evil. You need them for sustainable energy. If you need a boost, eat a wholemeal pitta and honey as an afternoon snack. You may find that, to your surprise, you're having to make a mental effort to eat *more* rather than less – more of the healthy stuff, anyway.

Cut down your portion size by using my idea and getting some smaller plates. Another handy trick is to tell yourself you'll come back for seconds but, once you've eaten, make it a rule that you'll wait ten minutes before you go back for more. Then ask yourself if you're still hungry enough for seconds. Most of the time, you really won't be.

If you can, take the time to enjoy your mealtimes. Try not to eat on the run, or on your lap while you watch TV. The reason is that you'll eat without thinking, and not thinking about what you eat is the road to disaster. The best way is to sit down at a table, eat slowly and really *enjoy* each meal. Think about it: three times a day at least, you get to eat something delicious that your body needs. So make the most of it and enjoy it. Food is precious, and we should value it. Pacing yourself at mealtimes will not only help you to enjoy your food more, it will also mean that you're less likely to overeat. Our brains don't receive the signal that we're eating and no longer hungry for a little while after we've started so, if you bolt food down, it's easy to keep feeding that sense of being hungry even when you're actually not.

Try not to load all of your eating on one particular meal in the day but aim for three well-balanced meals. And, never, never skip breakfast.

These are all important, but the biggest favour you can do for yourself is this: get moving. Get some exercise. Even if you don't want to lose weight, your body and health will benefit from it. If you do want to lose weight, it's non-negotiable. If you think you hate exercise, it's a sign that you desperately need to do some. If the gym isn't for you – and that's quite understandable, because it's not for everyone – there are plenty of other things you can do. Join a rambling club and go walking. Get a dog (a proper one that needs a proper walk) and take it out every day for a stride through your local park. See p. 169 for my exercise guide.

And don't tell me you haven't got time. If you don't believe me, add up the hours you spend watching telly or down the pub or whatever in the course of a day or a week. If you seriously can't find thirty minutes a day to go for a walk or a bike ride, then you need to think hard about how you can make changes so that you can, even if it means taking grumpy kids with you.

The whole point of this change in lifestyle is that it has to be sustainable and it has to be pleasurable, otherwise, you'll go back to your bad old ways and get fat. That means you may have to learn some new life skills – a bit of simple cooking, for example, so you can conjure up tasty meals at a moment's notice and avoid the temptation of the takeaway menu. Even throwing a potato in the oven to bake while you have a shower or read the paper is better than sucking down another plateful of cheap meat in a fatty sauce. And you might even enjoy it.

If you feel as if you're wavering, imagine the goal you're heading towards. Don't forget to reward yourself when you get to a new target, but try and make those rewards non-food- or drink-based. Go for a snazzy piece of clothing, a new book or CD, or a trip to the cinema.

The new you will be fitter, more energetic and look better in a suit. What's not to like?

Try not to be too influenced by those around you, particularly if they want to sabotage your new lifestyle. Some people will – it's strange but true. I think, for some, it's because they don't like anyone making the changes they know they need to make themselves but haven't got the will power for. For others, it's a challenge to break someone else's resolve. The best thing to do is not to talk about it, or have a handy excuse ready for when you're down the pub – 'I'm not drinking today because I caned it earlier in the week and totally overdid it …' – so that your mates don't see your not drinking as a challenge to get you sinking the booze. A friend of mine has a trick of ordering a drink and then leaving it almost untouched so that, when he is offered another, he points to it and says, 'I'm fine, thanks.' That's all right, if you can resist the temptation to down it. I don't know if I could.

When it comes to eating out, most restaurants do have healthy options. If in doubt, go for something simple – grilled fish and vegetables, for example – but beware of added creamy sauces. Remember, you no longer have to eat everything that's on your plate. It's perfectly okay to leave food which is likely to undo your good work.

Once you're in a restaurant or wherever, you just have to use your common sense about what to order and what to avoid. Go for dishes that are grilled, boiled, poached, steamed or stir-fried, rather than battered or fried dishes. Order fish or leaner meats – chicken, ham, beef – and opt for sauces that are based on tomatoes or vegetables rather than cream or cheese. Get your vegetables and salad plain and add dressing yourself – remember that dressing can double the calorie count of a salad. You can always request a plain vinaigrette if the dressing sounds too creamy. Don't forget that some salads made with couscous or beans can be really filling and delicious. You don't always have to go for the richest, meatiest option.

When it comes to pudding, it doesn't take a genius to work out that you should head for fruit, fruit salad and sorbets rather than cakes, rich puddings and ice creams. I try to eat either a starter and a main course, or a main course and a pudding. Glamorous ladies I know who eat out a lot often go for two starters and then share a pudding. They also avoid the bread basket and its tempting contents that you can all too easily nibble on while you're waiting for your food to arrive. I do that myself more often than not now, but if I do have bread, I'll pick something wholemeal or granary and eat it very slowly with only a tiny amount of butter.

If you're going for curry or a Chinese, whether as a takeaway or in a restaurant, you can eat very well without indulging in an orgy of calories. Go for plain steamed or boiled rice rather than pilau or naan bread, or egg-fried rice. At the Indian, order dry curries – tandoori and madras with chicken, prawns or vegetables – rather than ones made with coconut milk, cream or lots of butter (my favourite chicken korma is one of the worst offenders in that department). If you're eating Chinese, avoid the deep-fried food (spring rolls, battered prawns, sweet and sour pork, and so on) and plump for steamed fish, chicken chop suey, Szechuan prawns and stir-fried vegetables instead.

The same advice applies to a Thai restaurant – order plain rice and steer clear of anything deep fried and battered. Green and red curries also include a lot of calorie-rich coconut milk, so don't order these dishes too often and remember that steamed and stir-fried food is less fatty.

In an Italian restaurant, there are often lots of tempting creamy sauces on offer. If you're eating pizza, order one with lots of vegetables or a lean meat, like ham. If you're eating pasta, choose one with a tomato-based sauce and go easy on the added cheese. And don't be tempted by garlic bread – it's delicious but very high in calories. Bruschetta makes a lovely substitute: lightly toasted bread, often rubbed with a garlic clove, brushed with a little olive oil and heaped with fresh chopped tomatoes, olives and herbs.

As long as you keep a vigilant eye on what you're eating, and don't go out too often, it's perfectly possible to enjoy going out to eat while losing weight, or maintaining weight loss.

If you do give in and overindulge in some of the more calorific options – and why not, occasionally? – just remember that you'll have to make up for it with a couple of days of eating plainly and drinking lots of water.

Whatever you do, never think, Well, I've failed so I may as well go back to my old habits. That's defeatist talk and not worthy of the new you, the one who's decided to change and take control. Just acknowledge that you're human and fallible, but still determined.

Don't expect to see results tomorrow, next week or even the week after. Your weight-loss goals have to be long term and your lifestyle change permanent. You're much more likely to succeed if you dig in for the long haul and expect to lose weight over the course of months, or even a year, depending on how much you need to lose. It's realistic to lose a pound a week. It's utterly unrealistic, and dangerous, to lose 18lb in nine days, or whatever the internet may promise you. You can bet that any quick, major weight loss will be mostly water, and you'll simply put it back on again in no time. It takes a loss of 3,500 calories to burn one pound of fat. That's why reducing your intake by 500 calories a day and taking it slowly will be successful. Anything else is quackery and should be avoided like the plague.

Remember that it's better to be a little on the heavy side but fit and healthy than it is to be stick thin and inactive. So choose a realistic weight for you and go for it.

And that, ladies and gents, is how Fat Bloke slimmed. By the time you read this, I'll be a sylph-like thing of thirteen stone or just under. You won't recognize me! God, I won't recognize myself ...

It's been much tougher than I anticipated when I started. I've had to change my attitude to a lot of things. My basic principles were right, but I had no idea how hard they would be to put into practice, how much resolve I would need and how much help I'd need from others. I also changed my attitude to lots of things, from calories to internet chat rooms.

It's been a brilliant journey, too, enlivened immensely by the readers of my column and all their wild, wacky and often useful advice.

I look and feel so much better. I'm no longer worried that I'm about to keel over from a heart attack, which is a huge plus. And I know I'm doing my best to ensure that I'm around to see my precious kids grow up.

Fat Bloke's Golden Rules

Okay, here are my final, final tips. Whenever I'm flagging, I'll cast my eye over these and remember why and how I've done all this.

❏ **I am responsible for how I am. I can't blame anyone else, and it's up to me to change it.** If you haven't said this to yourself, you need to. It was only when I opened my eyes to what I really looked like and felt and realized that the only person who'd put food in my mouth and drink down my gullet was me that I was able to start making changes.

❏ **Listen to your body.** It's telling you all the time if you're doing the right thing or the wrong thing. If you feel down, tired, stressed or whatever, don't ignore it. Your body's asking you for something … Usually, it's asking for **more sleep, a healthy meal, less alcohol, more water and more exercise.** For god's sake, if you smoke, stop. NOW. I'm serious. You know, and I know, that it's a mug's game. It's like handing someone money to kill you slowly and painfully. Don't do it.

❑ **Take control.** Remember that no one is forcing you to eat or drink. The way you eat and drink now are simply habits that can be changed. I find it hard to believe that I really used to eat and drink the way I did. It seems blindingly obvious that getting fat was going to be the end result. I'm convinced I'll never go back, but I still need to stay in control of myself. Temptation is always out there …

❑ **Change your mindset.** Say to yourself, 'I'm not going to do the thing that's making me fat and miserable any more.' Don't approach it as a bleak existence of miserable denial – 'Oh, no, I've got to give up eating a packet of biscuits every day! Woe is me, what shall I do?' – but see it as something good and life-enhancing. You are making a decision to change your behaviour permanently, and that's a fantastic present to give yourself.

❑ **Nothing in excess, everything in moderation.** Balance up your life and learn to say 'no' and 'enough'. When it comes to immediate gratification,

I've learned to use my mind and really think about what I'm doing and whether it's really worth it. And, if I do give in, I know that I'm going to need to balance it out. A weekend of boozing means a week of restraint.

❏ **Don't struggle on alone.** It's hard to do it alone so, if you need help, ask for it. Lots of people are trying to do the same as you. The internet is great for this. There are on-line communities available day and night to offer support and encouragement. Often, your family and friends can't give that un-biased, simple pat on the back that you need. (Let's face it, some of your fatter friends might not even want you to succeed). If a slimming group or inter-net forum works for you, do it.

❏ **Real men watch their weight.** Fat, diet, calories, losing weight ... To me, this used to sound like something only women did. This book has been about a journey – my journey – and along the way I've had to face up to a lot of things I'd closed my mind to because I thought that, as a bloke, they didn't apply to me. The truth is that fat isn't about vanity and looks (well, maybe a bit), it's really about health. Men in this country are getting fatter and dying early because of it. We need to face up to it and embrace the changes that will save our lives and let us live to see our grandchildren.

I know I want to.

Thanks for reading this book. I hope I've inspired you! Good luck.

You have nothing to lose but your poundage.

Yours,

Fat Bloke

FAT BLOKE'S GUIDE TO GETTING FIT

You know, and I know, that exercise is vital. Even if you think you hate it, you've got to do it. Not only is it essential if you want to lose weight (unless you're prepared to live on 500 calories a day plus all the air you can eat), but it is also key to maintaining your health throughout your life. It's not just important for physical health, but also for your mental health and your concentration skills and intelligence.

If you're feeling pressured or depressed, a good walk will help lift you out of it. Exercise releases hormones that make you feel good and help to combat stress.

So it's a no-brainer really, isn't it? Use it or lose it, as they say. If you don't help your body by looking after it, you can hardly be surprised if it packs up on you. And then you'll be regretting all those wasted chances and opportunities. So start doing something about it NOW.

I did, and it's changed my life. I'm fitter, healthier, happier, brighter-eyed and generally more fun than I have been in years.

Let's Do It ...

Once you are over the age of thirty, you really need to think about how you're going to build keeping active into your life. Sad to say, you're already over the hill as far as your body is concerned – you're in the process of losing muscle mass and bone density. Before the age of thirty, it's relatively easy to maintain a healthy weight, because your metabolic rate is at its most efficient, so you can burn calories without much effort. BUT, if you don't build exercise into your life at this age, you will steadily gain weight which will be harder to lose as you get older and your metabolic rate slows down. I know – it's a real pain. Just as you start to care about your body and want to look after yourself, it gets a whole lot harder.

When you are between the ages of forty and fifty, your bones deteriorate faster than they are forming and your hormones change, making it harder to keep weight off. Over fifty, men lose their muscle mass fast, and it's often replaced by fat. It's more important than ever to get exercising to help preserve your health and fitness for as long as you can, and to ward off serious conditions, from heart disease to osteoarthritis.

At this point in your life, as your bone density and muscle mass are decreasing, you'll need to be careful and watch out for wear and tear on your joints. You're more susceptible to injury. Oh, and I should mention that the experts say you need fewer calories as well – around 150 calories fewer per day for every decade over the age of thirty. It just gets better and better, doesn't it?

What You Need to Do

Ideally, you should aim for two to four hours of aerobic (also called cardiovascular) exercise per week – that's around thirty minutes a day (and don't tell me you can't find thirty minutes in the course of a day) – and, if at all possible, another hour or so of weight and strength training. Aerobic activity is any sustained activity that involves large muscle groups and makes the heart rate increase and the lungs work harder to provide more oxygen for the body.

To burn fat, you need to get your heart rate up and maintain it at that higher rate for thirty to sixty minutes. Lots of people go out and start well but give up before they've reached that magical fat-burning period. For the first twenty minutes of aerobic activity, you'll be burning glycogen (or stored carbohydrates) so, if you stop after twenty minutes, you'll get some cardiovascular benefits, but you won't be burning fat. If you carry on for half an hour to an hour, you'll start using fat stores. Please don't think that means an hour of horrendous torture, because, if you think that way, you won't do it.

This should be fun and pleasurable and it will bring you many benefits, not least of which are:

- ❏ more energy
- ❏ less stress
- ❏ a fitter heart and lungs
- ❏ lower blood pressure

So, get your heart rate up and keep it raised for up to an hour. You don't need to push yourself to the limit, just get yourself puffed.

Easy Aerobic Exercise to Do Inside

- ❏ Dance around the room to your favourite music
- ❏ Climb the stairs a few times
- ❏ Do some vigorous cleaning, gardening or house-work (gets you fit, keeps the house/car/garage/lawn looking nice – what's not to like?)
- ❏ Get yourself a skipping rope and a bit of room to jump about in
- ❏ Try a fitness DVD or one of those interactive fitness programmes to use on a games console
- ❏ Get some home equipment – a mat, a step, stretchy bands, some small weights, a rebounder (or small trampoline, as they're otherwise known)

Easy Aerobic Exercise to Do Outside

❏ **Walking.** If you're just starting off or have joint problems or something that stops you doing more vigorous activity, try walking. A good brisk walk is a brilliant start – just try to get your heart rate up and maintain it for as long as you can. To give yourself more of a workout, try carrying some small weights. If you're relying on walking for all your exercise, invest in a pedometer and try to walk a minimum of 10,000 steps a day, building up to 16,000.

❏ **Jogging and running.** An excellent form of aerobic exercise and very effective (and cheap). You don't have to sprint a four-minute mile, and that wouldn't be the best way to burn off fat anyway. Just dig in and keep at it, puff away for as long as you can, but remember to get over that magical twenty-minute mark. It'll make you feel great, you know it will. Try and go out two or three times a week. Going with a friend will help keep you motivated.

❏ **Bicycling.** A lovely activity, especially in good weather. Just remember not to coast down too many hills – maintaining the movement and keeping the heart up is the key.

❏ **Dancing.** Try a salsa class or something similarly energetic. Don't forget that activities such as rowing and ice skating will get you puffed and provide some good aerobic exercise. Variety will help maintain your interest. Team sports will also help, but the amount of actual activity you do can be deceptive, as you may spend a bit more time waiting for the ball to come your way than you do chasing it. As I've said before, keeping going is the key.

Aerobic Exercise at the Gym

❑ **Treadmills, step machines, rowing machines, cycling machines, cross training ... it's all there.** You can switch on and get going. Just remember to start at an easy rate, and don't go at it all guns blazing before you're ready. Once you're comfortable and managing to get over twenty minutes' continuous exercise, keep varying your routine and upping your times/difficulty ratings, otherwise your body can become accustomed to a set workout and not work as hard as you'd like it to.

❑ **Classes.** Try an hour with a roomful of other people and an instructor. It will fly by, and it's often easier to get carried along when twenty other people are huffing and puffing next to you. Aerobic and body shaping are best.

❑ **The pool.** A great low-impact workout if you're starting out or suffer from injuries or joint problems. Relaxing, too.

Remember ...

❏ You'll need to warm up and cool down before and after exercise. Get an instructor at the gym to show you a few basic stretches.

❏ Listen to your body – if you think your joints are hurting or you're over-working, slow down or stop. Let the body recover between sessions, or you could risk injury.

Weights, Resistance and Flexibility

You might be under the impression that you only need to do aerobic exercise to lose weight. It's true that aerobic exercise is the best fat-burning activity. Weight training is anaerobic exercise, so it burns more glycogen than fat. But weights and resistance will help your metabolism so that you burn more calories when at rest. Not only that, resistance work will bring other health benefits as you get older, helping to strengthen your bones, skeleton and muscle mass, so you stay fit for as long as possible. Don't neglect this important area.

❏ The gym will have lots of resistance and weight-lifting equipment. Get a trained instructor to show you how to use the machines safely. Obviously, it's easy to injure yourself if you try and lift weights you're not ready for.

❏ Go to a Pilates or yoga class or try T'ai Chi – brilliant for relaxation as well as working on muscle groups and improving flexibility.

❏ At home, try lifting household objects: a bottle filled with water or sand; tins of beans; children.

❏ Work out a routine of press-ups, sit-ups, crunches and leg-lifts. Use stretchy bands or small weights from sports shops and, for one hour a week, do some resistance work. It might be worth investing in at least one session with a trainer who can show you what to do – it's important to do the exercises correctly.

Getting the Heart Pounding

As I've already mentioned, getting your heart rate up is really important.

I've found music is a great help in getting me moving and keeping me going. If you've got an iPod or a Walkman or a mobile with a music feature, you can make yourself an exercise playlist. Put on the kind of tracks that get you up and dancing at parties – preferably ones that remind you of being young, fit and active, because that's what you want to be again. It's also a handy tool because, if you put forty to forty-five minutes of high-energy music on your list, you know you have to keep moving for as long as the music's playing. Put on a slow track after forty-five minutes' worth and, when that starts, you'll know you can slow down and start cooling off. Then, when you're doing a forty-five-minute workout without too much trouble, you can – yes, you guessed it – work it up to an hour.

Here's some of the stuff I've got on my iPod: Stereophonics, 50 Cent, Earth, Wind & Fire, Eels, Deep Purple, Joe Jackson, Elvis Costello … and lots more. All feel-good, life-enhancing stuff that makes me want to get moving and keeps my heart rate up.

Here's a simple table to show you how far you need to raise it for a good workout.

To measure your heart rate, you can simply take your pulse at the wrist or neck. Every five or ten minutes, find your pulse and count the number of beats for fifteen seconds. Multiply that by four to come up with your heart rate.

Your age is a very important factor, and so is your general fitness and health. If you are a beginner, stay in the bottom of the range until you're able to move up more safely. If you have high blood pressure, you must consult a doctor before embarking on any fitness plan.

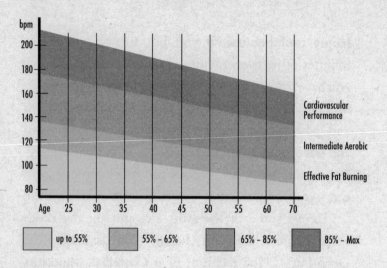

Good luck. You'll never regret getting started with exercise. You can only regret not doing it. So get out there.

FAT BLOKE'S GUIDE TO YOUR SHOPPING BASKET

You're going to lose weight. You're going to start exercising. You're making some big changes to your lifestyle, permanent changes. So why not look at changing the way you shop? The things you put in your shopping basket are the things you eat when you get home (um, bleeding obvious alert, but …) so if you only buy good, natural, healthy food, it follows that you'll only eat those things.

Well, all right, you might not if you have the local curry-house and pizza-delivery numbers on your phone, or live next door to a fast-food joint …

But you can do your best not to put temptation in your own way. Sometimes, despite your iron resolve, you may give in to it, that's only human. But try not to. If you love your takeaways too much to give them up (and I love them myself), allow yourself one night a week when you can indulge and, the rest of the time, aim for healthy home cooking.

Here are some useful ideas for going shopping.

The Supermarket Shop

Supermarkets do a lot of good, and the food they're selling these days is often top notch. It's not so long ago that you'd go into your local supermarket and find only some manky vegetables and frozen meat on offer, and not much else. Now, there is a great range, to suit every pocket, and plenty of convenient food to help make mealtimes much easier: packets of salad, ready-to-stir-fry veg, oodles of herbs and just about every fruit you can think of. Fancy some lemongrass, fresh ginger and chilli for a Thai curry? No problem. Passionfruit or blueberries to liven up your breakfast? Walk this way. And, in the meat aisle, you can find everything from your basic chicken to guinea fowl and venison as well as high-quality, free-range options. There are plenty of foods from around the world, and you'll find couscous next to pearl barley, not far from the noodles, rice and pasta. Our supermarkets offer us international eating now, and it's all there to be taken advantage of. It doesn't have to be expensive either: if you're cooking for yourself and your family, you can shop cannily and get lots of meals out of a fairly small shopping basket.

Even some of the ready-meals (and I'm not generally a fan) are a lot better than they used to be, though they're still not a patch on home cooking. Ready-meals are fine for when you really can't find the time to cook, but they should be avoided when you're watching your weight. Even if you're not watching your weight, try not to get into the habit of eating ready-meals too often. At the end of the day, whatever the quality, they are still processed food. Home cooking is superior in just about every respect, so try to train yourself to rely on what you make yourself for at least 70 per cent of your intake. Here are some reasons why:

❏ It's cheaper in the long run if you plan your meals properly and use leftovers for lunches, etc.
❏ It's better for you, because you can control your intake of salt, sugar and fat.
❏ It generally tastes nicer and is more satisfying. (Ready-meals are sold for profit, so they'll be low on expensive ingredients and high on cheap ones. They are often padded out with fillers and water, which is why you may still feel hungry after eating one.)
❏ It is actually fun to cook. Ask yourself what you do with the forty minutes you spend waiting for the oven to heat up and then the ready-meal to heat through … You could easily spend that time throwing together a few fresh ingredients for a delicious dinner.

Great though supermarkets can be, there is a bit of a problem with them. They are full of temptation, stuffed with bad foods. Have you ever noticed the way fresh food – fruit, veg, meat, fish, etc. – is outnumbered by everything else? Look at the tinned goods; the ready-meals and chilled, processed food; the frozen stuff; the snacks, biscuits, nuts, crisps, sweets, chocolates, cakes, doughnuts; the alcohol, sugary drinks and juices …

Bad food which tastes good is in supermarkets in spades, and you've got to close your eyes to it. That's hard, particularly if you've had bad habits before. Seeing it all laid out there for the taking and watching other people loading their trolleys with it can make it all seem fine and normal. But, actually, you don't need that plastic sack of crisps, or the calorie-laden biscuits or the family-sized boxes of treats. Sometimes, it's better not to see what's out there.

There are also those irresistible special offers and buy-one-get-one-free deals, which help you buy more than you need. It can take an iron will to walk past those, because everyone loves a bargain, right? But buying too much is one of the reasons why we are all throwing away so much of our food. In fact, it's better to have too little than too much.

So here are my tips for shopping:

❑ Get organized and make a list before you go. Plan your menus for the coming week, even if it's only roughly. If you wander about not knowing what you want, you'll waste your time and money by buying things you're not going to eat.

❑ Don't go shopping when you're hungry. You'll buy things because your stomach is telling you to.

❑ Take that list and don't deviate from it. Ignore all those tempting aisles devoted to bad food.

❑ If you buy a core of the same things from the super-market every week, see if you can organize an inter-net shop and delivery instead and try doing the rest of your shopping in local shops. It's true that it may seem more labour intensive than shopping in the supermarket but, the truth is, you're working pretty hard when you go to the supermarket. Think about it – going to the supermarket involves you driving there, and then spending at least an hour selecting all your food, wheeling it around, weighing your own fruit if you're buying it loose and bagging your own veg (if you don't do this, you end up being supplied with mountains of packaging). Then you have to unload your trolley and do your own pack-ing. It's slave labour in there! Letting butchers, fish-mongers, grocers and delivery men do all the work for you can be quite relaxing, and it doesn't have to be more expensive.

❑ Why not try shopping at a local food market now and again? You might believe that the supermarket is the cheapest place to buy your food, and that's what the supermarkets would like you to believe, but it's not necessarily true, particularly when it comes to fresh stuff. Most of the supermarkets' special offers tend to be on packaged goods and, while prices of staples, such as bread and milk and baked beans, are kept artificially low (they're known as 'loss leaders' – the supermarkets expect to make a loss on these products, but they will lure shoppers in), fruit and vegetables are often more expensive than they would be at a market. And, if you shop at the right time – the end of the day, for example – you can pick up bargains.

❑ If possible, seek out a greengrocer, a butcher and a fishmonger. I've found that using my local shops is a much more pleasant way to do the shopping, and I tend to buy only what I need rather than pile up stuff in a trolley without thinking about it. Don't forget, if you live in a town or city, local businesses often deliver as well, saving you time and keeping you out of temptation's way. The downside is that you have to carry a lot more – but think of it as useful exercise, or get one of those wheelie things that old ladies use. They do them in some nice trendy patterns now. You also might have to shop for food more than once a week, and that can be hard to fit into a busy schedule but, if you can do it, it is worth it.

❑ And the supermarket is always there if you need it!

Good Things for Your Shopping Basket

A lot of eating well is about changing your mindset. If you set out feeling gloomy because you're going to be deprived of all the sugar and refined carbohydrates you think you can't do without, you're bound to fail.

If you think instead: 'Yippee, I'm about to start eating a lot more healthy, delicious food which will make me feel great and look better!', you'll be starting off with a good, strong outlook. To me, dieting doesn't mean eating less. In fact, it probably means eating *more* – just more of the good things.

If you're planning some menus for the coming week, look at some of my meal ideas on p. 197 and flick through some cookery books. Try borrowing a couple from the library if you don't have any, or do a search on the internet. Delia's got her own website with a recipe database you can try out. Open your mind to eating something new. Think about it: most of us eat the same ten to fifteen meals *all the time*. We're in a rut. So just change your habits and eat different, healthier meals. Soon, that will be a habit too. At least, that's the idea.

Here are some ideas for things to put in your basket when you go shopping. If you pack some of these in every week (and then make sure you eat them, of course!), you'll be doing well.

Meat and protein

Avoid processed meats where you can. Good ham and other cold meats are fine, and bacon is a must, as it can add bags of flavour to your food, but steer clear of other prepared meat products.

❏ **Free-range eggs.** Eggs are a brilliant food. Excellent for a slightly heartier breakfast (poached or scrambled on toast), a quick lunch (cheese and spinach omelette, anyone?) or a comforting supper (can't beat boiled egg and toast soldiers on a cold Sunday evening).

❏ **Red meat.** Try and eat red meat only once or twice a week. Don't forget that cheaper cuts can be slow cooked to produce delicious and cheap casseroles, so don't think you always have to buy steak. Try braising beef, oxtail, mutton …

Lamb chops are great, but best if you buy them in season, from late spring through the summer. Delicious with a minty couscous salad.

Sausages can be fantastic, too, but make sure you grill them, and try to buy the best quality you can so that you get more protein, fewer fillers and less fat.

❏ **Game.** Game is often overlooked, but give it a go. Game birds are high in protein and low in fat, so try roasting quail, partridge, pheasant, pigeon … Rabbit is cheap and delicious. Venison is pricy, but can be absolutely gorgeous.

❏ **White meat.** Chicken and pork are good choices. My golden rule is to go for quality, so buy the best chicken you can afford. Roast chicken is one of the most delicious things in the world and, besides providing a family meal, the leftovers can go in sandwiches, risottos, pasta sauces … Pork chops make a quick, easy and tasty supper. Just make sure you trim the fat off.

❏ **Fish.** The most wonderful, healthy and delicious food (as long as we make sure we're eating it sustainably). See my recipe pages for some ideas. You ought to aim for fish twice a week. Try buying tuna steaks, smoked mackerel (excellent for lunch boxes or with salad), trout, salmon fillets or steaks, white fish or prawns from the fishmonger.

Fruit and veg

Your basket should have lots of this stuff in it. You can get sweet fixes from fruit, so get plenty in for puddings: strawberries, raspberries, blackberries, blueberries, lychees, passionfruit … you name it.

Don't forget bananas, apples, pears, and other fruits, which are good for snacks and to add variety and flavour to breakfasts. Kiwi fruit are a handy snack size, easy to carry and a delicious source of vitamin C.

For snacks, get dried fruit and nuts: dates, figs, cashews, apricots, Brazil nuts, walnuts, cranberries, mangoes, dried bananas, and so on.

Make sure you buy plenty of fresh vegetables for meals. Go for leafy green vegetables as well your standard peas and carrots. Don't forget that you can also buy frozen vegetables to keep in the freezer until needed, so you should always have an emergency supply on hand. For salads, I like cos lettuce or else mixed leaves with a peppery vibrant taste, like watercress and rocket. Young spinach and chard are also lovely. I chuck in everything I can to make an interesting and tasty meal: spring onions, cucumbers, pine nuts, avocados, celery, red peppers, cherry tomatoes.

Remember onions, garlic, carrots and celery – the classic base of many a great casserole, pie, soup and much more.

And a couple of large baking potatoes can be turned into a great lunch or supper.

Dairy

I'll buy yoghurt – there are so many delicious low-fat yoghurts around. I love some of the organic ones which come in flavours such as vanilla and lemon. You can also get soya yoghurt, if you want to pump up the heart-friendly factor a bit. You can use low-fat plain yoghurt in cooking instead of cream and mayonnaise.

I buy semi-skimmed milk. There's so much on offer now, including goat's milk, soya milk, rice milk – and even oat milk, which sounds kind of fun.

I get low-fat butter, but I don't buy margarines or spreads. That's just personal preference. I also don't go for low-fat cheeses (except low-fat cream cheese). I'd rather have a small piece of good-quality cheese than a block of tasteless substitute, but that's just me. To get the maximum flavour, I'll go for robust mature cheeses like real Cheddars and, of course, Parmesan.

I avoid ice creams and all dairy puddings apart from yoghurt when I'm thinking about my weight. Cheesecakes are definitely out, except on very special occasions!

Store-cupboard Essentials

Olive oil is a must for cooking – you don't need extra virgin for cooking in, that's best for dressings. Also sunflower oil. A little bit of butter is often great, but hold back if you can.

Tins – hurray for tins. Good things to have in tins in the cupboard include tomatoes and sweetcorn; tuna, sardines, salmon and other fish; baked beans; pulses such as chickpeas, lentils, kidney beans, borlotti beans, and so on.

You should also have your flavour enhancers on hand, as they'll deliver a lot of taste: anchovies, balsamic vinegar, Thai fish sauce, Worcester sauce, ketchup, sherry vinegar, tomato purée, mustards – French and English. Salt and pepper, of course, and good-quality vegetable bouillon or stock cubes. You can get good chicken stock cubes, which are excellent to have on hand.

You'll need pasta, rice (basmati and risotto rice, and brown rice) and some other grains, such as couscous or bulgur wheat.

Dried fruits and vegetables are great as standbys. I keep some dried mushrooms in the cupboard, which I can reconstitute for a risotto on a cold evening when the fridge is empty.

Don't forget your cereals and porridge oats for breakfast. I keep oatcakes and Ryvita on hand as well, for quick, low-calorie snacks when I hit a mid-afternoon low.

Obviously, there's lots more you can put in your shopping basket, and it depends on what you've decided to cook in any one week, but these are basics which I expect will be in your trolley more often than not. I know they're in mine.

What A Typical Weekly Shopping Basket Might Contain:

Dairy: Semi-skimmed milk
Natural yoghurt
Mature Cheddar, Parmesan
Low-fat butter
Eggs
Half-fat crème fraiche

	Low-fat mayonnaise
	Low-fat cream cheese
Carbs:	Wholemeal bread
	Wholegrain, sugar-free cereal
	Brown basmati rice
	Pasta
	Couscous
	Oatcakes
	Ryvita
	Porridge oats
Meat:	One chicken (for roasting, leftovers used to make a risotto or lunches)
	Stewing steak
	Pork chops
	Dry-cure smoked bacon
	Good quality sausages
Fish:	Salmon fillets
	White fish steaks
	Smoked mackerel
Vegetables:	Onions, garlic, celery, carrots
	Potatoes for baking and mashing
	Green leafy veg: broccoli, cabbage, spinach, courgettes, green beans
	Fresh basil, sage or whatever herbs you'll be using this week
	Mixed lettuces, cherry tomatoes, spring onions, cucumber, avocadoes

	Large red chillis
	Butternut squash
Fruit:	Fruit juice
	Apples, bananas, blueberries, kiwi fruit, grapes, satsumas, pears . . . whatever you fancy in fruit salads (and don't forget you can get fruit in tins, as long as it's not in syrup)
	Cooking apples
	Lemons
Dry goods:	Tinned tomatoes
	Tinned mackerel fillets, tinned tuna, tinned anchovies
	Tinned lentils
	Tinned mixed beans
	No-added-sugar baked beans
	Raisins, dried apricots, walnuts
	Frozen peas
	Wholegrain mustard
	Risotto rice
	Maple syrup
	Honey, peanut butter
	Stock cubes
	Dark chocolate

Here's a week's menu you could get from this shopping basket:

Sunday:

Dinner: Roast chicken with roast potatoes, carrots, peas and broccoli
Baked apples stuffed with raisins and apricots, with crème fraiche

Monday:

Breakfast: Cereal and fruit, fruit juice

Lunch: Wholemeal sandwiches with leftover roast chicken, lettuce, cucumber and a dressing of low-fat mayo mixed with mustard

Snack: Two Ryvita with low-fat cream cheese and a smear of honey

Dinner: White fish steaks, baked in the oven with basil and served with rice and mixed salad
Fruit salad and low-fat yoghurt

Tuesday:

Breakfast: Wholemeal toast with butter and Marmite, and a banana

Lunch: Tinned mackerel fillets in a mustard sauce with mixed salad or raw spinach and brown rice (can be mixed together earlier and eaten cold)

Snack: Peanut butter Ryvita

Dinner: Butternut squash risotto
Fruit salad and frozen yoghurt

Wednesday:

Breakfast: Cereal and fruit, fruit juice

Lunch: Hearty lentil soup and slice of whole-meal bread

Snack: Dried fruit and nuts

Supper: Pork chops (browned in a pan, then slow-baked and served with a basic tomato sauce and ripped sage leaves), with steamed cabbage and mashed potato

Greek yoghurt with blueberries and honey

Thursday:

Breakfast: Cereal and fruit

Lunch: Dry-fry some of the dry-cure bacon with an onion. Shred any leftover cabbage and add to the leftover mashed potato. Mix in the bacon and onion, and season. Can be heated through later in a microwave or grilled in the oven with a scraping of cheese on top

Snack: Oatcakes with cream cheese and cucumber

Dinner: Salmon fillets in lemon juice, oven-roasted with roast cherry tomatoes, anchovies and green beans, served with couscous

Low-fat lemon yoghurt and honey

Friday:

 Breakfast: Porridge made with water, with blueberries and a splash of maple syrup

 Lunch: Mixed bean salad with a small tin of
tuna

 Snack: Dried apricots and walnuts

 Supper: Nourishing beef casserole with lots of
vegetables, served with mash
Some squares of dark chocolate

Saturday:

 Breakfast: Scrambled eggs on toast

 Lunch: Leftover casserole on a baked potato

 Snack: Smoked mackerel paté (made with low-
fat crème fraiche and lemon juice) and
oatcakes

 Supper: Pasta in a spicy tomato sauce made with
bacon, chilli, garlic, courgette, and
sprinkled with Parmesan
Chilled kiwi fruit

Sunday:

 Brunch: Grilled sausages, poached eggs, baked
beans and toast

Note: you can buy good ready-made tomato sauces that
can be the basis of sauces for pasta, fish and meat. Add
these to your shopping basket if you don't fancy whip-
ping up your own, though it couldn't be easier: chop a

large onion and a fat clove of garlic and fry gently together in a tablespoon of olive oil until soft. Add a chopped chilli (minus seeds) if you want a spicy sauce. When the onion's cooked, add two tins of tomatoes (plum or chopped) and bring back to the boil, then simmer gently for as long as you like but until the tomatoes have broken down. The flavour will get richer the longer you cook it, though you may need to add a bit of water if it gets too dry. Add a teaspoon of sugar, a pinch of salt and some black pepper. Whizz in the blender for a smooth texture, or leave as it is.

FAT BLOKE'S MEAL IDEAS

Breakfast Ideas

Breakfast is a really important meal and shouldn't be skipped. It wakes up your metabolism and gets it working, it delivers the energy you're going to need for the first part of the day, which is often busy and demanding, and it will give you calories to work off as you go. There is an old saying that runs, 'Breakfast like a king, lunch like a rich man, dine like a pauper' – the idea being that you load up your calorie intake to the early part of the day, when you're using energy, rather than to the end, just before you switch off and go to sleep. I think it's better to eat moderately throughout the day, but you can certainly afford to give yourself a good start first thing. A filling breakfast will help prevent those mid-morning dips and the craving for something to eat. Adding some fresh fruit can push up the health factor as well.

❑ **Cereals, crunchy oats, muesli, Weetabix, etc.** You aren't going to be surprised when I tell you to avoid the sugar-coated varieties and, where possible, to go for wholegrain versions. There are some really delicious, healthy cereals on the market, and you can pep them up with more fresh fruit – sliced banana, blueberries, strawberries, melon, etc. – and a spoonful of natural, low-fat yoghurt. Try soya yoghurt if you want to add some more heart-friendly protein.

❑ **Porridge.** If you have memories from childhood of gruesome porridge, try to forget them. On a winter's morning, a big bowl of hot porridge made with water and semi-skimmed milk, and sprinkled with a little bit of brown sugar and maybe some fruit, is a brilliant breakfast. It's so easy to make, incredibly filling, very comforting and delicious. There are instant versions if you're not quite confident enough to go it alone with a bag of rolled oats, but it's easy, I promise.

❑ **Toast.** If you're going to eat toast, go for the wholegrain version, and try some of the heavier varieties. Most brand-name and supermarket loaves are very light, and that's because they're full of air. Artisan and traditionally baked bread is much heavier, not because it's stale but because it's got more actual bread in it. You'll need two or three slices of the light stuff to fill you up, and that means more butter and whatever else you eat on top – and you'll feel hungry again quickly. Denser bread will fill you up better and for longer. Go for low-fat butter if you can (it's up to you if you want those low-calorie spreads. I don't, but that's just me), and avoid jams and marmalades packed with sugar. You can get low-sugar versions.

❑ **Eggs.** What a brilliantly versatile food. They're great for breakfast, lunch or supper (and some people do indeed follow all-egg diets, though I wouldn't recommend that). Although they're high in choles-terol, they are a great source of protein and vital nutrients. A poached egg on wholemeal toast is an excellent breakfast. You can also scramble (beware too much butter) or dry fry in a non-stick pan.

❑ **Cooked breakfasts.** There's nothing wrong with something hot first thing. Beans on toast is a filling and nutritious breakfast. If you want the full English on the odd occasion, or at a weekend, go for it. But …

❑ Choose back bacon, not streaky, and grill it

❑ Avoid sausages, or have just one and grill that, too

❑ Add a lovely grilled tomato

❑ Eat wholemeal toast, not fried bread

❑ Scramble or poach the eggs rather than frying them

❑ Avoid frying mushrooms in lots of oil. Use a non-stick pan with a spray of olive oil or grill field mushrooms

Of course, there are masses more things you can eat for breakfast. The main thing is to keep an eye on the fat content, because you'll be eating lots more calories than you need without noticing it if everything is slathered in butter. Just don't forget to eat breakfast, that's all!

Lunch Ideas

It may be that, like me, you eat your lunch in a canteen and have a choice of hot and cold food. If so, what you choose all comes down to what suits you best. Beware of making the mistake I was making – eating two large main meals a day, because I was having a big cooked meal in the middle of the day and another when I got home in the evening. You can still eat a cooked meal, but go for a light version if you're eating in the evening too. Fish is a great option here, because it's lean protein, with lots of excellent extras that our bodies need.

Lunch is a superb time to add some extra vegetables and greenery. You may have to change your mindset a little. The main thing is to get away from sandwiches. They're fine once in a while, but there are so many other lunches you can eat which will provide more for you. Shop-bought sandwiches can be low on the good stuff you need and packed with fat and unnecessary calories so, if you do like your lunchtime sandwich, think about making your own, with decent wholemeal bread, plenty of fresh salad and some lean meat, cheese or whatever takes your fancy.

Otherwise, look at investing in a wide-necked thermos so that you can take hot soups and casseroles into work.

If you are buying your lunch, try things other than sandwiches. How about sushi? Good protein, filling and tasty. And lots of coffee shops also sell hearty soups to take away.

Here are a couple of my favourite lunches. If you're at home and making a quick lunch for yourself, try:

❑ **Omelette.** Whisk three eggs together, and add a pinch of salt and a grind of pepper. Put a drop of oil or a bit of butter in a small non-stick pan and warm up on a medium heat. Pour the egg mixture into the pan and let it set. As it's cooking, you can add whatever bits and pieces you fancy, for example, some chopped ham, mushrooms, a handful of grated cheese, chopped spring onions, spinach. Cook to your taste – some like it runny, others not. The bottom should be golden-brown. Slide out of the pan, and fold over, if you like.

❑ **Soup.** A good hearty soup full of delicious things will fill you up nicely. Add a roll, or slice of brown bread, and follow it with a piece of fruit or cheese and you've got a great lunch going on. You can buy lots of good ready-made soups. Try and go for the ones with plenty of filling extras: beans, pasta, lentils, chickpeas, barley, and so on. These are good, slow-release sources of energy and provide the carbs and protein you need. You can make your own if you're feeling inspired, and you can whip up a soup very quickly with whatever odds and ends you have in the fridge or the store cupboard.

Quick lentil soup. Chop one medium onion and fry in a bit of olive oil in a medium-sized saucepan over a medium heat until softened. Add a chopped carrot, a chopped clove of garlic, and maybe a chopped chilli if you have one on hand and like a bit of spice. Cook for another five minutes, stirring occasionally. Drain a can of lentils (you can also use dried lentils, but, if they are the kind that need soaking, you'll have to do that the night before) and add to the onion mixture. Make up stock from a good-quality cube, or granules – it can be vegetable or chicken. You'll need about a pint, maybe a bit more. Put the stock into the saucepan, making sure that the lentils are covered. Bring to the boil and simmer gently for about ten minutes. Then, either use a hand-held blender, or pour it into a blender, and whizz it all up. Taste for seasoning, and add a bit of salt and pepper if it needs it. All done – a filling soup in about fifteen minutes flat.

❏ **Baked potato.** If you can think ahead and get organized, pop a potato in the oven to bake for an hour or, better, an hour and a half, before you want to eat it it. Bake at about 180°C. You can fill it with anything you like: salad, hummus, baked beans, cheese, coleslaw, tuna mayonnaise, curry ... Just don't use too much.

❏ **Couscous.** This is a great and versatile basis for lots of different lunches. It goes well with smoked fish, or freshly cooked fish. Also, it's delicious with roasted vegetables, fresh herbs and feta cheese. You can make this the night before to take in to work.

❏ **Pasta and rice.** You can make a very filling, low-calorie lunch based on pasta or rice. Try and avoid adding fat and, instead, go for vegetable sauces. I'm always partial to a bowl of pasta with some lightly steamed green veg and a spoonful of pesto. Some chopped anchovies can add a punch of flavour. A bit of grated Parmesan on top is fantastic, just don't go mad with it.

❏ **Bean salad.** I like to experiment with these, and I've stumbled on some really tasty combinations. You'll be surprised what a good lunch can come out of a tin of beans. I take a tin of whatever takes my fancy – chickpeas, kidney beans, borlotti, butter beans, etc. – and add some chopped softened onion, or raw spring onions, and then a bit of whatever I can find. Some chopped tomatoes, celery, grated carrot, fresh spinach ... whatever there is around. Then I'll empty in a small tin of tuna, some smoked mackerel, or I'll fry up some chopped bacon. I've even been known to slice up some anchovy fillets and add those. You've got to give it a good burst of flavour, or you won't enjoy it as much. I'll dress it with a light vinaigrette or even a tiny bit of mayonnaise. If you'd rather not use mayonnaise, try some low-fat crème fraîche or yoghurt. Very nice.

❏ **Tins of fish.** While I generally don't go in for tins and processed food, I make an exception for fish. Some brilliant and useful things come in those tins. John West do a good light lunch based on tuna with a couple of extras. You can also get mackerel or herring fillets in a variety of sauces, so quick and easy to eat with a bit of rice and maybe some salad veg. Don't forget the good old sardine, a really tasty lunch or light supper on some hot toast. Tinned tuna can be made into a great salad (see above for one example), or mixed with some nice crunchy veg, dressed with a bit of olive oil or mayonnaise and eaten in a pitta bread or on a baked potato. If you've got some mashed potato left over from the night before, you can mix in a tin of salmon, a squirt of tomato ketchup, a teaspoon full of English mustard, a drop of fish sauce or anchovy ketchup and some salt and pepper and make yourself a fish-cake. Fry it lightly in a dash of oil to colour it and then oven bake for about twenty minutes at 200°C. Eat it with a big serving of salad or some spinach, raw or cooked, as you like.

Another favourite of mine, for lunch, a weekend brunch or a light supper, is kedgeree. If you've never had it before, look it up. It's a simple dish of rice cooked in chicken or fish stock, with onions, boiled eggs and fish. The purists do it with smoked haddock, which is fantastic, but you can always improvise with a tin of salmon.

And talking of salmon …

❑ **Fresh fish.** If you haven't done it before, you'll be surprised at how quick and easy it is to cook a fillet of fish. One of the quickest lunches I know is to pop a piece of salmon into a roasting pan – put a bit of olive oil down to stop it sticking, and season lightly – then put that in the oven at a high heat – 220°C – for about ten minutes, while I get some vegetables or salad ready. By the time I've done that, the fish is cooked. Delicious, filling and healthy. You can also put a fillet under the grill, about ten minutes each side, depending on the thickness.

❑ **Smoked fish.** Smoked mackerel is so tasty. Add it to a salad, and you'll be amazed how satisfying it is. You can mix it with a low-fat cream cheese, plus a dash of lemon juice and a teaspoonful of horseradish, for a delicious pâté which you can eat on oatcakes or Ryvita with cucumber and tomato. Yum. Hot smoked trout and salmon are also great to flake into salads or eat with some veg on the side – easy to take into work as well.

❑ **Ryvita.** Classic diet food, and yet I really love Ryvita, because they can taste so good with the right stuff on them. Try chopping a good handful of rocket and cherry tomatoes. Shave in a few pieces of Parmesan, then dress lightly with a little olive oil and balsamic vinegar. Load on to two sesame Ryvita. Brill. I also love tomatoes with feta cheese dressed with olive oil and vinegar. Fabulous. For a sweetish treat, try honey on the Ryvita, and then slices of banana. Obviously, don't eat too much of that.

❑ **Leftovers.** Great for lunches, and cheap. If you roast a chicken at the weekend, take off all the meat and use it over the next few days for sandwiches and salads. Leftover casserole or mince can be fantastic with that baked potato, a bit of rice or on some hot toast. Cold pasta might sound unappealing, until you call it pasta salad – then it's fine!

Dinner Ideas

You're at home and cooking for yourself, and you don't want to do anything too fussy or fancy. You just want something quick, healthy, filling and tasty. Well, I want to give you a few ideas. Here's one of my favourites:

❑ **Chicken noodle soup.** You'll need a wok for this one, and some exotic herbs, which you should be able to find in the supermarket. Lime leaves are in the dried-herb section. Chop some garlic, ginger and spring onions. Heat up a teaspoonful of sesame oil in the wok and, when it's nice and hot, fry the garlic, ginger and spring onions quickly, for about thirty seconds. Then add a pint of chicken stock, then bash a stick of lemongrass and throw that in, along with a couple of lime leaves. Shake in a couple of drops of nam pla, the Thai fish sauce, and a finely chopped, deseeded red chilli. Let it simmer. Meanwhile, chop a chicken breast into small pieces, and some more spring onions. Throw the raw chicken into the simmering stock, along with the whites of the spring onions, and let it poach for about seven minutes. Add some noodles, and cook for a further three or four minutes until the noodles are done.

It's a delicious and filling soup which you can

adapt by using prawns instead of chicken, and adding pak choi.

On the whole, my dinner ideas are simple. When I'm trying to lose weight, I avoid eating refined carbs, particularly at the end of the day. There may be no rhyme or reason to it, but I find I'm more satisfied with a plate of lean protein and lots of vegetables or salad. I prefer not to feel stuffed these days, so I'll eat something like:

- ❏ **Pork chops.** Brown in a frying pan and then cook slowly in the oven at a medium heat in a covered pot with a splash of cider
- ❏ **Lamb chops.** Marinate for half an hour in a bit of olive oil with chopped garlic and rosemary, and then grill
- ❏ **Chicken breasts/thighs.** There are about a million things you can do with chicken, and it's a great source of protein. I love it lots of different ways. Chicken thighs marinated in lemon juice and garlic and then baked in a 200°C oven for twenty-five minutes are a favourite. Grilled chicken breast is good for you but can be a bit dull. You can add some excitement by smothering it in a sauce of low-fat yoghurt mixed with some spices and then cooking it in a hot oven for twenty-five minutes.

Chicken's also great wrapped in Parma ham, speared through with a stick of rosemary, and roasted

❏ **Game birds.** They're quick to roast and full of flavour. Here's an idea: Take two quail per person. Stuff each one with a mixture of fresh breadcrumbs, thyme, chopped dried apricots, with a splash of olive oil to bind. Put a piece of streaky bacon over the breasts and roast in a hot oven at 200°C for about twenty-five minutes

❏ **Fish.** You can have a meaty fish such as cod or the cod alternatives, such as pollack, and eat it with lentils and bacon; or a light fish such as trout, which I like to stuff with slices of lemon and dill, wrap in foil with a splash of white wine and then bake for thirty minutes. Salmon is always a winner – a grilled salmon steak with a dab of butter and some steamed veg is always good

Make sure to add a good variety of vegetables: broccoli, crunchy green beans, broad beans, peas, carrots, spinach – whatever your favourites are. If you're having potatoes, remember to have some leafy green veg as well. You can replace potatoes with sweet potatoes and roasted butternut squash if you feel the need for a bit of variety.

The best thing you can do is flick through a recipe book, get yourself one of those slimming magazines with all the excellent low-calorie recipes, or take a look around a forum on the internet. Lots of people are sharing ideas out there. Try and use this opportunity to get out of your eating rut and explore some new ideas.

FAT BLOKE'S GUIDE TO NUTRITION – SOME EASY FOOD FACTS

Here's some really basic stuff ...

Energy and Food

The energy we need in order to live comes from food and drink, specifically from fat, carbohydrate, protein and alcohol.

❏ If you take in more energy than you expend, you will gain weight
❏ If you take in less energy than you expend, you will lose weight

Calories

To me, they used to sound girly but, actually, calories are the best way to decipher food and find out how much energy it supplies our bodies.

Calories are a measurement of energy. There is a complicated explanation of how it's all done but, luckily, there are plenty of physicists out there doing the hard stuff for us. All we need to know is that a calorie is a useful little piece of information. A gram of carbohydrate (starch or sugar) provides 3.75 calories; a gram of protein provides 4 calories; a gram of fat provides 9 calories, and a gram of alcohol provides 7 calories. You'll have noticed that alcohol contains nearly as much energy as fat (which is where I was going wrong for so long. Imagine swigging a couple of wine glasses full of butter every night – that's equivalent to what I was doing).

Where we get our energy from is important, as food doesn't just supply us with the power to maintain our body functions (breathing, organ function, and so on) and move about but also gives us the tools to grow and repair tissues. Food supplies the nutrients that are the building blocks of a healthy body.

The amount of energy any person needs depends on a variety of factors: age, sex and lifestyle are the main ones.

When you consume more energy than you need, it is stored in the body in the form of fat. But I expect you knew that!

Obesity

The facts about obesity are sobering, to say the least.

The number of both adults and children who are overweight and obese is increasing all over the world, and this brings all those associated health risks that now sound so familiar: cancer, heart disease, stroke, type 2 diabetes.

According to the British Nutrition Foundation (www.nutrition.org.uk), in the early 1980s, 6 per cent of men and 8 per cent of women in the UK were obese. In just twenty years, those figures have skyrocketed. The latest figures for Great Britain show that 42 per cent of men and 32 per cent of women are overweight (i.e. have a BMI between 25 and 30), and 25 per cent of men and 20 per cent of women are obese (their BMI is over 30).

And, while adults are bigger than ever before, the number of obese children is increasing too … Now, over one in five boys and one in four girls is either overweight or obese, according to the BMI standard. As you'll know from earlier in the book, I have my doubts about the application of the BMI to measure body fat, but it turns out that the other ways of measuring body fat – with tape measures – also reveal that Britain's children are getting fatter. A study by Dr David McCarthy, a senior lecturer in human nutrition at the London

Metropolitan University, found that the average waist-band measurement of two-year-old girls has increased by more than 5 per cent in a decade. The equivalent measurement in boys has increased by 4 per cent. That means that our children may be even fatter than is indicated by studies using the BMI. We ought to be extremely worried about this. Children need to grow up with healthy attitudes to food, nutrition and exercise, or what hope is there?

The British Nutrition Foundation reports that 30,000 deaths per year in England are obesity-related. But obesity also causes chronic diseases which ruin lives and cost all of us money in care and treatment. The World Health Organization has predicted that global obesity will mean that there are 300 million people with type 2 diabetes by 2025.

Don't let you or a member of your family be one of them.

The British Nutrition Foundation reports:

> It is not just a problem of excess fat, but where that fat is deposited. People who have extra weight (fat) around their middle – 'apple shaped' – are at more risk of some of these diseases than those who have most of the extra weight around their hips and thighs – 'pear shaped'. Because the health risks of obesity are compounded by the influence of fat

distribution, waist: hip ratios or waist circumfer-
ences are now commonly measured. In general,
men are at increased risk of obesity-related diseases
when their waist circumference reaches 94cm (37
inches). For women, risks increase at 80cm (32
inches). The risks of disease become substantially
increased at 102cm (40 inches) for men and 88cm
(35 inches) for women.

Being overweight (BMI 25–30), but not obese
(BMI greater than 30), also poses increased risks to
health, and it is important that people in this cate-
gory should not put on any more weight and
ensure that they are physically active, make sensi-
ble dietary choices and do not smoke.

Your Energy Intake

This will vary depending on your height, sex and
weight. The government guidelines are that women
require an average of 2,000 calories per day, and men
require 2,500. But this is only a rule of thumb. You can
best work out what your intake should be by calculating
what your ideal weight is, and increasing or reducing
your intake to help you reach it. See below for a chart
showing the ideal weight for men. It's based on the
Body Mass Index, and I find it a bit on the light side,

but I would say that, I suppose ... Apologies if you're over 6 feet 2.

Remember, it takes a deficit of 3,500 calories over a week – or 500 a day – to burn one pound of fat. So you'll need to create a deficit by eating less or doing more in order to lose that one pound.

Ideal Weight for Men (based on Body Mass Index, optimized for men)

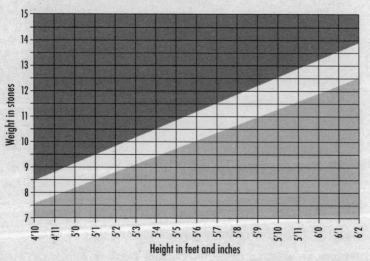

Anyone whose body fat is more than 20 per cent above the desirable range is likely to be line for those obesity-related nasties: coronary heart disease, type 2 diabetes, gallstones, arthritis, high blood pressure and cancer.

The Importance of Eating Well

Your body wants to survive and thrive. It really does. That's why it can sometimes appear to have no problem coping with all the things you throw at it, from excess alcohol to fat-drenched takeaways. When you're young, you stay thin more easily, cope with your hangovers and can't ever see a time when you're going to be falling to pieces. But, eventually, this bad treatment will take its toll on your body, and you'll start to see and feel the damage.

Your body needs fuel to live and if you give it that fuel in the form of fatty, sugary, processed foods, it will manage to carry on. You could feed yourself only on chips and chocolate and still be able to get up in the morning. God knows that there are parts of the world where people are surviving on very little indeed.

But the result will be that you'll probably die young. That's what happens to the malnourished. If your body hasn't received those vital chemical building blocks that keep it healthy, you'll gradually deplete any resources you have, and then your body will be very weak and vulnerable to disease. And your immune system won't have the ability to fight in the same way it would if it had the right minerals and vitamins.

Brutally put, that's why people die young in places where there is not enough food, or where the food sources are nutritionally deficient.

So, while, theoretically, you could get all your calories from bad foods which are high in sugar and fat and still survive, there are lots of reasons why that's a bad idea. Your body and your brain will work best on a diet with plenty of fresh food, vegetables of all colours, lean proteins, essential fats and oils and carbohydrates. The British Nutrition Foundation has come up with some recommendations for people who want to change their diet:

❑ Eat more starchy (carbohydrate) foods, such as bread, potatoes, rice and pasta, but avoid adding fat to these foods, or not very much. Eating them in wholegrain versions is the best way, as they will release their energy more slowly. You'll also get fibre, excellent for the system.

❑ Eat more fruit and vegetables. Aim for five portions a day, excluding potatoes, and, as with the carbs, don't add so much fat that you undo some of the good. Strawberry ice cream isn't exactly a portion of fruit, is it?

❑ Choose leaner cuts of meat, and don't add a lot of fat when you're cooking. Once you realize how many calories there are in oil and butter (there are about 80 calories in 10g of butter, and you can easily spread that on one piece of toast if you're not careful), you'll want to be a bit more sparing with fat. Cheese is delicious, full of calcium, and can add great flavour to food. Just don't eat a block of it in one go.

A Healthy Diet

You should choose a variety of food from these four food groups every day:

❑ **Bread, rice, wholegrains, pasta, potatoes. Also yams, breakfast cereals, oats, noodles, maize, barley, bulgur wheat, couscous, cornmeal, and so on.** These vital dietary building blocks provide energy, B vitamins, calcium, iron, fibre and folate for red blood cells.

❑ **Fruit and vegetables, including leafy green vegetables. Fresh, frozen, dried and tinned fruit and vegetables all count. Also, pure, 100-per-cent fruit or vegetable juice and smoothies count (as long as they *are* pure).** You'll get vitamin C, fibre, folic acid, carbohydrates and carotenes needed for growth and development from fruit and veg.

One medium piece of fruit, such as an apple or orange, a slice of melon or two satsumas, would count as a portion. Three tablespoonfuls of cooked vegetables would count as a portion, or a small bowl of mixed salad. A serving of juice will count as one portion, but you should only count juice as one, no matter how much you drink. You will still need to eat other fruit and vegetables to get the requisite fibre.

❑ **Milk and dairy foods such as cheese, yoghurt, fromage frais and soya alternatives. (Butter, eggs and cream are not included.)** Dairy food provides calcium, zinc, protein, vitamins B12, B2 and vitamin A. All of this is vital for growth and repair in the body. You need around three servings a day, and you can use low-fat alternatives as well.

❑ **Meat, poultry, fish, eggs and other non-dairy sources of protein. This includes meat products such as burgers and sausages, and tinned and frozen fish. Pulses also come in the category of proteins, although they do not provide quite enough zinc, and no vitamin B12.** From this food group, you'll get protein, iron, B vitamins, zinc, magnesium and omega-3 fatty acids. Once again, this is all necessary for growth and repair as well for blood cells, nerve function and energy.

Eat moderate amounts of this food group, and trim off excess fat. Aim for two portions of fish a week, one of which should be oily (salmon, mackerel, trout, sardines or fresh tuna).

Alternatives to meat include tofu, nuts,

mycoprotein, textured vegetable protein, beans and pulses.

❑ **Fats and sugars.** Butter, margarine, oils, cream and anything containing a lot of these things (such as fried food, cakes, biscuits, ice creams, crisps, rich sauces, gravies, and so on) are fats. Soft drinks, sweets, jam and more of the usual suspects (cakes, biscuits, puddings) are sugary. As is sugar itself, of course.

These foods provide very little nutrition, although fats are essential to the body, so you mustn't try and cut them out entirely. Instead of animal fats, choose olive oil, rapeseed oil or sunflower oil. Remember: you'll find essential fats in fish and nuts. Try to cook with as little fat as you can. Sugar adds flavour and sweetness but is very high in calories and decays the teeth. You can buy low-calorie sugar and use sugar substitutes. Some people like diet versions of fizzy drinks.

Remember, too, to cut down on salt – adults should not eat more than 6g a day. Salt is vital, though, so, again, don't try and cut it out completely.

Keep up your fluid intake – dehydration can often be mistaken for hunger, so it's a good idea to keep drinking. One and a half to two litres a day is recommended for adults in this country, though much of that will come from your food. Between three and eight large glasses of water is plenty to keep you hydrated. Tea, coffee, juice, squash, and so on also count, but they can have a dehydrating effect, so make sure you drink at least one glass of pure water every day.

Your diet should provide you with enough vitamins and minerals, but there are dietary supplements available, if you wish to use them. If you are taking anything other than a multivitamin, it's best to ask your doctor beforehand. Your doctor can also offer tests that can determine whether you need supplements or not.

TEN COMMON DIETING MYTHS

My friends at the British Heart Foundation have been a great help in giving me good information for healthy eating that will reduce my risk of heart problems.

They've also reminded me that it's easy to fall prey to some diet misconceptions. I've certainly been taken in by a few of these in the past, so I'm listing them here, just in case you've heard these myths and thought that there might be something in them.

1. Skipping breakfast is a good way to lose weight

Skipping breakfast will make you feel tired and hungry during the morning and encourage you to reach for high-fat, high-calorie snacks. In fact, people who eat breakfast are more likely to maintain a healthy weight that those who don't.

2. The stricter the diet the more successful it will be

If you eat nothing but grapefruits or oranges all day long

for a week you will, of course, lose weight. But fad diets that drastically cut calories will quickly become boring and won't be effective in the long run. It's not necessary to starve to lose weight. Making small changes that you can stick to is the key to long-term success.

3. You have to give up your favourite foods

Depriving yourself of all the foods you enjoy won't work. You'll eventually give in to temptation and abandon your efforts. There is no harm in allowing yourself a treat now and again.

4. Eating at night makes you gain weight

It doesn't matter when you eat if you are eating too much – a calorie is a calorie at any time of the day! It is healthier for your digestive system not to eat a heavy meal before you go to bed but a later dinner will not make you any fatter than an earlier one.

5. It is possible to spot-reduce, or to lose fat in one part of your body

As unfair as it may seem, we can't pick and choose from where we gain or lose weight. When the body loses fat, it is lost throughout the body. Focusing on one area of the body when exercising may develop better muscle tone in that area but it will not remove more fat.

6. Certain foods, such as grapefruits or celery, can burn fat

No food can actually help you to burn fat. Some foods with caffeine may speed up your metabolism slightly for a short time but they won't cause significant weight loss.

7. Carbohydrate-rich foods, such as bread and pasta, are fattening

It's calories that count and gram for gram carbohydrate has less than half the calories of fat. But carbohydrate-rich foods can be fattening because of the fillings and toppings commonly added to them – such as creamy sauces on pasta and butter or cheese on baked potatoes. Some carbohydrate-rich foods, especially wholegrain versions, are packed full of fibre which can keep hunger at bay. For example, wholegrain bread is more filling than white bread and will keep you satisfied for longer.

8. You shouldn't snack between meals

Eating healthy snacks between meals can actually help you to control your appetite and keep your blood sugar level steady. Fruits and vegetables are a great choice.

9. Low-fat means low-calorie

Replacing fat with other ingredients can still result in a product with a high calorie content. Don't be fooled – check the label. Quantity is also important – you won't cut back on calories if you eat twice as much of a low-fat product as a full-fat one.

10. You have to exercise intensively to burn fat

Even low intensity exercise will burn fat. Walking, gardening or doing housework will help you to burn calories and lose weight.

So there you have it. Remember that a healthy, balanced moderate diet where you take in less calories than you burn up will cause you to lose weight. There's nothing else to it.

Good luck, and get eating!

USEFUL INFORMATION

For general health:

British Heart Foundation: www.bhf.org.uk

British Nutrition Foundation: www.nutrition.org.uk

NHS: www.nhsdirect.nhs.uk

MaleHealth: www.malehealth.co.uk

Men's Health: www.menshealth.co.uk

BBC: www.bbc.co.uk/health/mens/_health

Men's Health Forum: www.menshealthforum.org.uk

For calorie counting:

www.weightlossresources.co.uk

For information on alcohol:

www.alcoholconcern.org.uk

www.drinkaware.co.uk

www.units.nhs.uk

Books:

I Can Make You Thin – Paul McKenna

Cook Yourself Thin – Eastwood, Erskine, Henley, Michell

The Food Doctor Ultimate Diet – Ian Marber
Jamie's Ministry of Food – Jamie Oliver
How To Cook – Delia Smith

Magazines:

Slimming magazine
Health and Fitness magazine
Good Health magazine
Men's Health magazine

ACKNOWLEDGEMENTS

To Sam for making it a reality. To Kate and Becke at Penguin, and Kirsty, for all their hard work. To the readers of my column, all the practitioners who have been so generous with their time and expertise, Tig and the British Heart Foundation team, Clare and the team at Cardio Direct, Imran my trainer and Justine at the *Daily Mail*. Thank you everyone.

live more

If you would like to receive more information on Healthy
Penguin titles, authors, special offers, events and giveaways,
please email HealthyPenguin@uk.penguingroup.com